How Bullets Saved My Life

Fun ways to teach some serious writing skills

Judy Green

Foreword: David Booth

Pembroke Publishers Limited

© 2010 Pembroke Publishers
538 Hood Road
Markham, Ontario, Canada L3R 3K9
www.pembrokepublishers.com

Distributed in the U.S. by Stenhouse Publishers
480 Congress Street
Portland, ME 04101
www.stenhouse.com

We acknowledge the financial support of the Government of Canada through the Book Publishing Industry Development Program (BPIDP) for our publishing activities.

We acknowledge the assistance of the Government of Ontario through the Ontario Media Development Corporation's Ontario Book Initiative.

Library and Archives Canada Cataloguing in Publication

Green, Judy
   How bullets saved my life : fun ways to teach some
serious writing skills / Judy Green.

Includes index.
ISBN 978-1-55138-255-5

   1. English language—Composition and exercises—Study and
teaching (Elementary). I. Title.

LB1576.G744 2010 372.62'3044 C2010-903826-6

Editor: Kat Mototsune
Cover Design: John Zehethofer
Typesetting: Jay Tee Graphics Ltd.

Printed and bound in Canada
9 8 7 6 5 4 3 2 1

FSC
Mixed Sources
Product group from well-managed
forests and other controlled sources
Cert no. SW-COC-002358
www.fsc.org
© 1996 Forest Stewardship Council

Contents

Foreword

Where was this book when I began teaching a Grade 5 class in Hamilton so many years ago? I taught creative writing on Tuesday at 2:30, often using a calendar picture of something like autumn leaves. My students wrote their compositions, and then I edited them for spelling, and they were copied onto foolscap sheets with straight pens dipped in blue-black ink. There was almost no instruction by me, and no questions from them. It was some kind of ritualistic experience conducted for each class in the junior wing; those students who could, did, and those who couldn't, didn't. It never occurred to me that writing was happening in all the other subjects, that composing and constructing ideas and opinions was going on every time a pencil or a pen or a keyboard made a mark. Writing is an act of thinking, representing, constructing, rethinking, formatting, illustrating, revising, and sharing; as teachers, we need to be alongside our students with all the bits and pieces that can motivate them and support them as they explore and develop their writing selves.

In this new book, Judy Green offers us fine help as writing coaches, encouraging us with her own life stories and connecting them to practical suggestions for actually guiding youngsters into knowing about how writing works, and how they can make use of the tools and techniques that effective writers have in their repertoire. I think the most difficult assignment we give our students is "Write whatever you want…" Most of us need some help focusing our thoughts so that we can move ahead, turning ideas into print that somehow represents what we envision in our minds. Judy knows this process of initiating ideas for our writing and presents us with a schema for battling writer's block. Because of her deep and comprehensive background with children's literature, Judy makes significant connections between what students read and what students write, reminding us of the symbiotic relationship of these two literacy processes.

There are so many features of writing support offered in this excellent book that, after reading it through, I wanted to find that Grade 5 class and shout: "I know how to do it now!" We need to reveal to children the secrets necessary for writing in different genres, for different functions, so that students can write as researchers, reporters, scientists, poets, storytellers. Judy helps us with organizational issues, with finding ways to add our voice to the texts we construct, with adding the details that breathe life into the words, with selecting words that matter and expressions that add new dimensions. And in this era of multimodes, she discusses when and where conventions are appropriate in creating different text forms.

I greatly appreciate her ideas for the bugbears of revision and editing; she understands this complex process and leads us through with practical hints. And Judy knows the importance of how final copy looks, how it can affect the readers—and the writers, when their work looks professional and represents their personal best.

When Judy compares learning to write with becoming better at a sport, as coaching can move a child forward in both these areas of learning, I resonate with her analogy; I saw my son grow into a fine hockey player with superb and skilful coaches who knew how to help him in small increments, focusing on each particular growth point in his development. Judy offers us this mandate for nurturing young writers; she helps us to acquire and implement the tools of the trade, from fiction and nonfiction to fonts and forms. We have come a long way as writing teachers, thanks to educators like Judy Green. Read her book, and teach well.

David Booth
2010

Preface

As a child, I lived north of Toronto. My grandparents often invited me to stay for weekends in the city. My grandmother taught elementary school and enjoyed writing poetry. She read her latest poems to us at every visit. I remember them vividly. Like all writers, she got her ideas from many places—nature, family members, unexpected events, interests, feelings, and real life.

Proudly, my grandma got a poem published in a Grade 4 reader called *Ready Or Not...*, an anthology of short stories and poetry for children. I did not realize it then but, looking at the book now, I see my grandmother was in good company. Other contributing writers included the distinguished Judy Blume (author of *Are You There God? It's Me, Margaret*; *Blubber*; and the five *Fudge* books), Jane Yolen (author of *Owl Moon* and *How Do Dinosurs Say Goodnight?*), Eve Merriam (reknowned for her light-hearted wit in poetry, fiction, and nonfiction), and Astrid Lindgren (creator of *Pippi Longstocking*). Jack Booth edited this collection.

Around the time my grandma's poem was published, I attended university. I earned a degree in English literature and then enrolled at the Faculty of Education, University of Toronto. That move made sense. My mom was a trail-blazing elementary school principal (one of the first-ever female principals in her county) and my dad taught high school and college.

One day at the Faculty, our language arts instructor said, "Come to class tomorrow. We have a guest speaker." Not surprisingly, many of us felt overburdened with due dates at that point. Nevertheless, after we found our seats the next afternoon, Dr. David Booth arrived. David is a Professor at the Ontario Institute for Studies in Education of the University of Toronto, and is one of the world's leading experts on literacy. I remember his talk about reading and books. He got us thinking about learning, language, and wordplay. By the end of his talk, we understood we'd heard the voice of an exceptional man.

Since then, I have heard David speak on many occasions—no less spellbinding. I wish all teachers had that opportunity. Every time those able to downshift into his cool ambience and dreamy tempo drink deep, they come away spiritually replenished. David Booth is relentless and relentlessly solemn—a great speaker in the full joy of his passion. He has won awards in Canada and the United States for his teaching and writing. I consider myself fortunate to have had the opportunity to learn lessons from him. Through years of professional development workshops, literacy conferences, receptions, and dinners, David continues to inspire me. And, yes, he is the brother of the anthology editor Jack Booth. Small world.

I started my career as a teacher. But the truth is I love books. So when Scholastic Canada offered me a job as a Book Club Editor, I jumped at the chance. That experience taught me the business of writing, editing, and publishing. Since then, for the past 20 years, I've worked in private practice as a children's book editor, writer, conference speaker, and workshop leader at hundreds of schools. I spent 15 years as the editor of a national annual guide to the best children's books. My connection with so many exceptional authors has given me insight toward the writing process. As well, I am a mom. My son has a unique view of the world, and I continue to learn from him. These experiences enrich my understanding of the reading–writing connection.

At one of my professional development workshops, the teachers and I discussed writing. Later the principal e-mailed me to say it was both affirming and motivating: "We have a good staff, but many teachers aren't as confident about literacy as they would like."

Teaching writing is complex. We need to know the elements of good writing (content) and the mechanics of writing, including punctuation, capitalization, and spelling. At times, the two interconnect. This book focuses mainly on the elements of good writing. These elements apply to both narrative and expository writing—fiction and nonfiction.

Because writing involves many skills, some teachers approach it with trepidation. Their expertise may lie in another area—geography, computers, history, and more. Recently, I spoke at a Teacher/Librarian conference. Every librarian invited one teacher from his or her school to attend. At the end, a teacher came to speak with me: "Thanks for your session. You've inspired me. I have a math degree. Until today, I felt so unsure about how to teach writing."

Another time I had a casual conversation with a family friend. He graduated in political science and education. Now, he was embarking on a teaching career with a split Grade 5/6. "I have no idea how to teach language arts," he panicked.

Let's face it: most elementary teachers are responsible for several subjects—math, science, music, physical education—not just language arts. You have many programs on your mind. Unlike being a ski instructor, or a swimming coach, you have more than one focus. No wonder some people are apprehensive about teaching writing. We can only be dexterous in so many areas!

Ski instructors are experts in their field. They are so passionate about snow that they do everything possible to share their love of the sport with those they teach, even under adverse conditions: ice, freezing rain, frigid temperatures. They never try to teach everything at once. Instead, they break down skills into simpler bits. They use terms that children understand and show by example how to perform each skill. For instance,

> "Watch how I bend my knees."
> "Notice my shoulders always face downhill."
> "See how I plant my pole at the ski tip?"

Beginning skiers learn with instructors that demonstrate, awe, and inspire. Over time, they put the little things together and move toward proficiency. Teaching writing is like ski instructing, in that we present each lesson separately and break down skills into simpler parts. We strive for terms that kids understand and we show by example how to accomplish each skill. And, in both cases, we must be responsive to all the unplanned teachable moments that arise.

You don't have to be an expert writer to teach writing. But if literacy—the ability to read and write—is your mandate, you do need to know the qualities of good writing in order to make (amazing) connections between reading and writing. Luckily, we have wonderful children's authors to use as role models. They are the experts that demonstrate, awe, and inspire.

You can be an excellent writing teacher by exposing your students to the best books possible, and using them to demonstrate specific skills. Read and reread books aloud, pointing out *how* authors do particular things. For example,

"Listen to how the author starts this story."

"Notice the alternatives to *said.*"

"Look at how the author uses his senses to describe things."

"Listen to the voice in this passage."

"Pay attention to the nouns and verbs in her sentences."

When you read aloud to students, and show *how* the author writes, you're teaching writing.

For most of us, writing is hard work. It's highly creative and involves many things to think about: clarity, a strong lead, voice, grammar, word choice, organization, details, description… even good endings. Thinking and writing go hand-in-hand. We need lots of thinking time to do a good job.

Writing is a craft. For me, it's like a construction project. I hone the craft of writing in the way that a carpenter hones the craft of a building. By understanding the theory, using good tools, and following a plan, I, too, build a structure. I want to share these tools with you so that your students can build their own stories.

With gentle urging, Mary Macchiusi, President of Pembroke Publishers, nudged me to write this book. She felt I had something important to share with readers. I must confess, however, that I was stuck before I even started. The thought of writing another book overwhelmed me. My mind wandered during the hours I stared at the computer, choosing words and constructing meaning. Yet as I battled structure and struggled with organization, I relished the creativity of writing.

After I got started, I realized that I do have a lot of information for teachers, but I didn't want to make the reading too long. I was having trouble moving ahead and including everything I wanted. Then I decided to use bullets to add material without burdening the reader. Bullet points keep people reading. They highlight easily-digestible bits of important information, keep attention focused, and break up dense pools of text. Used properly, bullet points are clear, concise, and to the point. I found the bullet points helped me get on with writing effectively and efficiently. They did—if not literally "save my life"—give new vigor to my work. The title *How Bullets Saved My Life*, with its exaggeration and playfulness, creates interest and illustrates playing with words. (I like creative and whimsical book titles when they are appropriate. They add a bit of life and fun to the structured and serious side of writing.)

Writing skills are critical to academic success. More than ever before, math and science are language-based. Most employers care about writing skills. In a labor force full of mediocre writers, someone who writes well stands out.

Some children dream that one day they might even become published authors. If your students read a lot, write a lot, and follow tips from other authors, that happy ending just might be theirs.

Introduction

Imagine: 60 kids you've never met before, sitting in front of you, facing a backdrop of award-winning children's books. On a typical day, I lug three boxes of literature in a variety of genres—including picture books, novels, poetry, nonfiction—into schools. I use books to make reading/writing connections throughout my workshops.

"Who is your favorite author?" I ask kids at the start of every session. They mention authors of classic books like Roald Dahl and newcomers like Mélanie Watt, creator of the hugely popular *Chester* series (Chester-mania is exploding in English-speaking countries).

By inquiring about students' favorite authors, I learn lots from their answers. Better yet, *they* get reading recommendations from each other. Eventually it helps me lead them from being readers to writers.

As we discuss many favorite writers, I steer our conversation toward the authors' books. "What do you like about their stories?" I ask.

"They make me laugh."
"There's lots of adventure."
"They're interesting."

Kids talk about book characters as though they are mutual friends. Easily, this activity has been the source of wonderful discussions.

Ultimately, we want to make our writing *interesting*. Good writing is always interesting to read. In my workshops, we develop a shared common vision about the elements of good writing. Those elements include

- a catchy title
- interesting details
- a great lead
- word choice
- presentation

Under the heading *What is Good Writing?* I list these elements on large lined chart paper. Then, using their favorite authors, I show kids how they can make writing interesting. These strategies apply to *all* kinds of writing—fiction and nonfiction.

Interactive white boards are common in education, but chart paper appeals to me because it becomes a permanent record for the group. Kids can go back to it and reread the page when they need to.

"I like Robert Munsch," young kids say. They enjoy naming titles by him. I explain that Robert Munsch tells his stories aloud many times before he writes the words. And that most of his ideas come from everyday life. I'm glad they mention Robert Munsch, because we can use his books to teach a variety of writing lessons:

- Getting ideas from daily life
- Rhythm and repetition in language
- Good story starters
- Catchy titles

Let Authors Help You Teach Writing

When I ask older students about their favorite authors, many mention J.K. Rowling. I explain how she fills Harry Potter books with hidden meanings and word-foolery. (One year, the editor of *Kidsworld* magazine asked me to write an article about the hidden meanings in Harry Potter.) I tell them about the time my son's Grade 5 class did a three-month author study on J.K. Rowling and saw her read in Toronto. I went as a parent volunteer. Imagine: 15,000 kids dressed as wizards at the largest literary reading ever.

Before J.K. Rowling came on stage, popular author Kenneth Oppel read from *Firewing* as a warm-up act. Students like Kenneth Oppel. His award-winning *Silverwing* series and other adventures (*Airborn*, *Skybreaker*, and *Starclimber*) galvanize readers. Unfortunately, that day, we could hardly hear Kenneth Oppel read in the city's cavernous baseball stadium. Beside me, 11-year-old Meredith grumbled about the noise. She owned all of Kenneth Oppel's books and had brought them with her to follow along. Finally, in exasperation, she yelled out to the crowd, "SHUT UP! I'm trying to hear him!"

What makes Kenneth Oppel such a great writer? He is a master of description. As one boy explained to me, "He makes you feel like you're right *there*." Often I'll ask kids, "How many of you have ever written something, then your teacher asks you to add more description?" Sure enough, most raise their hands. We can use Kenneth Oppel's books to help teach lessons on

- descriptive language
- sensory details
- setting
- using similes
- writing with nouns and verbs

Kids look up to their favorite authors as powerful role models. Good books carry students to new realms of the imagination; we can use them to teach elements of good writing.

As a child, I loved to read. My mom took me to the library every week and read to me every night. My dad encouraged us to read any books in our house. We had one rule: we could watch only one hour of TV a day. In those days, except for TV and radio, we had no other electronic distractions.

Back then, few of our picture books came in full-color. Most drawings were "black, plus one"—meaning black ink plus one color. Think *Millions of Cats* by Wanda Gag, *Make Way for Ducklings* by Robert McCloskey, *The Five Chinese Brothers* by Claire Huchet Bishop and Kurt Wiese, *The Story of Ferdinand* by Robert Lawson, *The Carrot Seed* by Ruth Krauss, or the original versions of Curious George.

At school, we read from a book called *Developing Comprehension in Reading*, a collection of numbered short stories. As a kid, I had no idea what that title meant, or why the publisher highlighted the "C" word in red ink. All I knew was that, every day after lunch, the teacher would assign a story number (they had no titles). After we read the story silently to ourselves, we turned to the next page and answered ten comprehension questions. Everything bored me about the book—its cover, pictures, and numbered stories. Yet we worked through this series from Grades 2 to 6. In those days, we paid little attention to authors and illustrators. No authors ever visited schools or had blogs where we could read and write about their work.

Kids today are lucky! They have great authors from which to choose. Many of their favorite writers have amazing websites with blogs, book news, biographies, teaching guides, and contact information. Here's how author Richard Scrimger (author of *The Nose from Jupiter* and *Bun Bun's Birthday*) greets visitors to his home page: "Hi there. How you doing? Welcome to the site. Come in and make yourself at home." In addition, authors visit schools and give talks to students, teachers, parents, and librarians.

Recently, I visited a school in Cookstown, Ontario. As I finished working with the primary children, a Grade 1 girl marched up to me.

"Do you have a website?" she asked.

"Yes." I said.

"Okay, what's your number?" she demanded. I admired her confidence and eagerness. Apparently, she loves learning tips and techniques from authors who are willing to share.

Many picture books are world-class—tuned to perfection. Use them in all grades as models to teach a variety of writing lessons. Get to know the ones with rich language such as *Song and Dance Man* by Karen Ackerman, *Owl Moon* by Jane Yolen, and *The King's Taster* by Kenneth Oppel. Equally, we have fantastic novels, nonfiction, and poetry books for children. They make great teaching tools. Young writers need continual nourishment from expert writers.

This book looks at how to use good literature as models for teaching writing—ways you can help students become good writers. When we show *how* authors approach specific skills, kids see themselves as insiders to the process and rise to a new level of sophistication in their work.

Have the Right Stuff

When I worked as the editor of *Our Choice*, Canada's national annual guide to best books for children, I collaborated with the Canadian Children's Book Centre and a freelance designer. Every year, the CCBC's Library Coordinator shipped all the new books—about 700!—to my office. One of my roles involved writing annotations for the guide.

One spring when the books arrived, my son and his friend Michelle helped me sort and load them onto shelves. For me, the best part of the job meant watching their reactions to new books. "What kind of reading do you like best?" I asked Michelle.

"Oh, you know—science fiction, fantasy, horror… and teen angst," she smiled. To capitalize on students' interests a teacher can

- Give students excellent models to teach writing.
- Get an assortment of books for every interest; link reading to current trends and students' personalities.
- Talk to kids about what's good.
- Listen to what they like so you can motivate them.
- Learn who their favorite authors are (and why) so you can suggest other books they might enjoy.

Recently, a principal invited me to do a writing workshop with her staff. I asked each teacher to bring along two or three of their *students'* favorite books. We would discuss how we could use them as writing models. One Grade 8 teacher expressed her dislike of fantasy and science fiction. When she said, "You couldn't pay me to read a Harry Potter book," I winced. Regardless of *your* interests, kids need to read and explore various forms of writing. Knowing different genres helps children in their writing.

In 2009 I attended a literacy conference lead by David Booth at Nipissing University. He has received an honorary Doctor of Education there and is collaborating with the faculty to create an international centre of research excellence in literacy. At that conference, David celebrated language—"Hooray for wordplay!" He highlighted children's books—picture books, novels, poetry, and nonfiction—where "words sing on the page." He emphasized that the more kinds of text kids read, the stronger writers they will be.

I encourage teachers to stay abreast of best books. They're part of popular culture. I discover many new-to-me books in my discussions with kids. But the ones you recommend do not always have to be trendy or brand new. Many are "day-olds," but still tasty." They can still teach us lots about good writing. For example, if your students like Harry Potter, they might enjoy *The Dark is Rising* sequence by Susan Cooper.

Google "If You Liked Harry Potter" for fantasy lists galore!

Books are like meat. Some need to marinate. Some need to be around awhile before they settle in. Nor must all book covers be glitzy—with shiny letters and embossed blood—to be appealing. David Booth recommends *The Lorax* and *Charlie and the Chocolate Factory* for wordplay. Dr. Seuss first published *The Lorax* in 1971. For those concerned about the environment, it has become a popular metaphor. British author Roald Dahl published *Charlie and the Chocolate Factory* in 1964.

When my son was in Grade 8, his teacher asked the class to read any title by Farley Mowat, and write a book report. Farley Mowat is one of Canada's first published authors. We had many books in our house, but nothing by him, so this assignment required a trip to the public library. Since my son likes humor, I recommended *The Dog Who Wouldn't Be*. Thankfully, Cory enjoyed it. After that, I suggested *Owls in the Family*. On our third library visit, Cory signed out every Farley Mowat book he could find: "I love this guy!" he grinned. What's good about Mowat's writing? His stories are fast-paced, gripping, personal, and conversational. He's famous for poetic descriptions and vivid images.

Every year from September to June I do school visits. As well, teachers and principals ask me to do professional development workshops. In dozens of districts, administrators say the same things:

"We have been concentrating on the writing process and would like an in-depth workshop to zero in on particular skill development."
"Our School Growth Plan focuses on writing and on improvement in that area."

In my workshops, I set up a display of good children's books for the audience. Experts and mentors, people who love their craft and want to share it, write these books. During our session, I help connect students with their favorite authors as mentors.

As teachers and kids swarm into the library, they comment on the colorful assortment of picture books, fiction, and nonfiction. Even older students enjoy discovering a favorite picture book. "I love Jillian Jiggs!" they gush. I smile, because picture books are for people of all ages, not just little kids. They are a literary art form. At all grade levels, we can learn about writing when we study good picture books.

My student workshops begin with a discussion of good authors. Sometimes, this sparks so much interest I wonder how we'll get to the next segment. As kids declare their favorite writers, I watch their peers' response. A few names crop up time and again. Inevitably, whenever someone says "Roald Dahl," others nod in agreement. Along with *Charlie and the Chocolate Factory* and *The BFG*, they love *Matilda*.

In that novel, Matilda Wormwood's parents have no interest in their daughter. They pressure her to watch television instead of read. Matilda, undaunted, reads every children's book in the library. She takes revenge on her parents through a series of pranks. Kids love Roald Dahl's jokes and the "nastiness" in his stories. Luckily, in real life, most parents today realize that reading is fundamental to school success. Now the audience for my workshops has grown to include parents.

The more kids read, and the more we (adults) read to them, the more they learn about writing. Good authors teach kids new words, ways to start stories, ways to end stories—even how to think of a catchy title. Teachers view writing as a process that develops along with other language skills, like speaking and reading.

Yet when it comes to the older grades, some teachers admit that they don't have time for reading aloud. Sadly, some librarians say older students rarely visit the library. And many parents stop reading to their children as soon as they can read on their own.

More than an isolated activity, writing is part of a multi-pronged program that includes

- reading aloud to students at all grade levels
- posting lists, wall charts, and examples of descriptive writing
- recommending good authors and giving writing tips in classrooms, on school websites, through PA announcements and newsletters
- writing daily
- offering access to author's websites, writing forums, and book blogs

Since reading and writing go hand-in-hand, good programming also features

- book-sharing activities and peer collaboration
- focusing on *how* writers get ideas and shape their text
- genre reading and response
- displays of student writing
- involving parents and celebrating writing

When writing is your focus, make every effort to encourage kids and other members of the school community to join in the reading–writing connection. These are the driving forces of motivation.

Writing Traits

After launching the concept of good writing with kids, I guide our conversation toward them being writers:

Now it's your turn. Pretend you are going to write something. What's the first thing you need to have?

The answer, of course, is an "idea." After our discussion of idea development, we talk about organization. I show them storyboard sketches as one organizational tool. I read aloud the first few lines of books to demonstrate how writers start stories. Then we move to the other elements of good writing.

I design my workshops based on my knowledge of the writing process. Several authors and illustrators contribute original manuscripts, sketches, and storyboards. Often teachers say it ties in with the writing traits. In the 1980s, a teacher team identified six writing traits to help students look at their own writing. This model refers to characteristics of writing and creates a common vision of what good writing is. Since then, another trait has been added to the model, resulting in 6+1 traits. I use the model as an organizational tool for this book because it helps break writing into manageable parts. The writing traits are

1. Ideas
2. Organization
3. Voice
4. Word Choice
5. Fluency
6. Conventions
7. Visual Presentation

I like this model because that's how people write. We begin with ideas, add details, and then try to organize them. Once we have a plan, we say things in our own voice. We choose the best words and make the sentences flow. Then we concentrate on the conventions and presentation. When we work in this order, ideas come before conventions. Why focus on punctuation or spelling if the details are confusing?

The writing strategies and activities in the chapters that follow will help struggling students as well as strong students. These ideas reflect my experience. You can adapt them to your program. My first book, *The Ultimate Guide to Classroom Publishing* guides teachers through all aspects of the publishing process. This one focuses more on the reading–writing connection. Whether you are an experienced writing teacher, or want to feel more sure-footed about your craft, I hope this validates what you know about the process, offers insight, and lifts your learning in many new ways.

1

Getting Ideas

> *Pretty much everything inspires me. Events, people, our society, past, memories of my childhood, funny situations, interesting places, animals and more.*
> —Mélanie Watt (author of *Chester* and *Scaredy Squirrel*) (Watt, 2008)

"Where do you get your ideas?" That's the number-one question writers get asked. Ideas form the content and main theme of any piece of writing, together with the details that enrich and develop that theme. Several things inspire authors to write stories. Some read books to get ideas, some tell stories of their families, and some create fantastic worlds from their imagination.

"Please focus on generating ideas for writing." Principals typically send this e-mail to me. And rightly so. Ideas are the core of every piece of writing. In fact, our ideas and content are the *reasons* for writing.

Many kids have trouble thinking of ideas. They see their lives as uneventful and think of themselves as boring people. Ask them what they're interested in, and they shrug and say "I don't know." Some kids feel as though they have to think of a grandiose idea or a funny story, when in fact the opposite is true. Often their best ideas come from ordinary life, and are serious stories.

Many children fear writing. They look at an empty screen or a blank sheet of paper and say, "I don't know what to write." Other kids have so many ideas swirling around in their heads that it is hard for them to focus on just one.

Sometimes, young writers make the mistake of choosing big topics such as "My Life," "School," or "Sports." Topics that are too big or too general can easily become overwhelming and unfocused. Students have better success when they narrow down a topic and focus on one aspect of it—one experience, one event, or one memory—in detail. This helps them replace generalities with specifics and makes their writing stronger.

When I do school visits, I explain to kids that, as we begin writing, we generate ideas. All writing should convey a message and be easy to follow. As we develop a list of ways authors get writing ideas, a strong sense of awareness emerges in the students. Soon, the kids feel empowered to make these strategies their own.

Then we look at the nuts and bolts of developing good ideas. Ultimately, this list includes

- What is your message?
- Is it focused and clear?
- Do you include important details relevant to your topic?
- Is your writing interesting and easy to understand?

Teachers need to help students find and develop good writing ideas. If your students struggle with developing writing ideas, adding details and staying focused, this chapter has some tips for you.

Where Do Writers Get Their Ideas?

Everyday Life

"My ideas come from ordinary, everyday life," says award-winning author Jerry Spinelli (2000), author of *Maniac Magee, Loser, Crash,* and *Wringer.* Often the best stories come from our daily lives. Help your students understand that they are all interesting people and they all have interesting stories to tell.

Everyone has different experiences and perspectives. Encourage your kids to write stories based on experiences from their own lives. Explain that the words they choose and the way they string them together are unique. Imagine writing about things you have never done before or know nothing about.

Repeatedly, authors tell children, "Write what you know." As award-winning children's novelist Betsy Byars says, "The words *author* and *authority* go together. When you write about what you know, you write with authority. Authority is the greatest gift a writer can have."

When you write about something familiar, you already know lots of details. See Add Interesting Details on page 34.

Writing about Moments

CBC broadcaster Stuart McLean helps students confine topics from everyday life and get beneath the surface in their story. McLean writes a weekly radio show and taught writing at Ryerson University. One of his favorite classroom times occurred when he asked his students to write something he called Moments ("Story Exchange"). Here is how he explained it to them:

Write a story. There are two rules: Your story must be true and it must be short. After that, it is up to you. Write about a moment that you have experienced, witnessed or heard about. Something funny or something touching—anything. It might be a moment of kindness or a moment of cruelty... a moment you are proud of, or ashamed of. It might not even be about you. It might be about someone you know. Or maybe it's about someone you don't know at all... maybe it's something that made you smile or cry.

Something has to happen in your story. Some feeling or emotion has to be lurking behind it. If you succeed in finding such a moment (and you will, because our lives are full of these moments), you will move the reader.

Write about big things and small things. Usually the most important things are small things. Write about funny things and sad things. How short? Two paragraphs, or two pages. Or more, or less. Just put your story on paper. Use simple short words. They are the best kind. Think of it as writing someone a letter.

I've seen wonderful results using this strategy. Writing Moments helps students stay focused and give exquisite details. In addition, it takes the pressure off having to write funny things. Many kids think they have to write humorous stories. Help them understand that good writing can be serious in nature. Nine-year-old Cory writes about a solemn moment that made him proud. His story begins:

On July 10th, I was the ring bearer at my cousin Cynda's wedding. This meant that I had to carry the diamond ring successfully down the aisle…

A few years later, Cory wrote about another Moment: a true story about an event that happened when he was twelve. See Rescue at Gold Point on page 97.

Encourage your students to think about moments in their lives. Do they remember the day their brother or sister was born? Or the time their family took a special trip? What do they recall about a favorite birthday party? Moments like these provide good opportunities for descriptive writing. When kids write true stories based on something they have experienced, witnessed, or heard about, they already know many details.

Robert Munsch has written more than 50 picture books, including *The Paper Bag Princess*, *Class Clown*, and *Smelly Socks*. What do kids like about his stories? "They're funny!" *We Share Everything!*, for example, captures a primary teacher's sweet and patient efforts to instill the code of sharing—along with a big dose of Munsch fun. But as I explain to kids, "Not everything we write has to be funny. In fact, *trying* to write in a humorous way can be difficult, unless it comes naturally. Some of the best writing focuses on serious stuff."

Most of Robert Munsch's ideas come from everyday life. They touch on things kids can relate to: wiggly teeth, bad hair days, sharing… And they help give kids focused story ideas from their own lives. For example, read *Andrew's Loose Tooth* to students, then ask, "Who has ever lost a tooth in an interesting way?" This encourages lively discussions. Or read *Aaron's Hair*, then ask, "Who has ever had a bad hair day?" Many kids have stories about that too. Or try *We Share Everything!*, then ask, "Who has to share something with someone?" Many heads bob up and down. Soon, children realize that they all have stories to tell, based on ordinary everyday life.

I get a big response with that approach. Recently, at a literacy conference, writer and educator David Booth said, "Literacy is really about response." When I see the way kids respond to Robert Munsch's stories, I see huge opportunities for oral storytelling, and for reading and writing connections.

Books

"READ. Read like a wolf eats," advises Gary Paulsen, one of the most important writers of young adult literature today. At a young age, Paulsen developed a passion for reading—and the taste for adventure that makes his novels so real. This master storyteller has written more than 175 books and won Newbery Honors for *Hatchet*, *Dogsong*, and *The Winter Room*. His novels often appear on Best Books lists.

Most good writers read a lot when they were young. Reading plays a fundamental part in developing good grammar and writing skills. A friend of mine who grew up in Montreal once told me he was in the 98th percentile (meaning he was better than 98 percent) of those writing the matriculation exam in English. Recently, he elaborated on that in an e-mail: "Point to notice is that I developed my writing skills by reading over 50 books in a Grade 6 competition to beat Nancy the class brainiac."

Books also help kids relate to ideas. In *Franklin Fibs*, the turtle says he can eat 76 flies in the blink of an eye. Knowing how young children enjoy rhymes, I jokingly ask them, "How many of you would *try* a piece of *fly pie*?" Every group has risk takers—girls and boys. This leads to another idea: Yucky Food stories. Kids love talking about swallowing slimy creatures, eating ladybugs, and sampling dirt. In *My Sister Ate One Hare* by Bill Grossman, a girl eats snakes, ants, and other things—but peas make her nauseous. I point out that often things we read about remind us of stories from our own lives.

Many writers try their hand at fractured fairy tales where they change the details of a familiar story. Popular books like *The True Story of the 3 Little Pigs!* by Jon Scieszka help inspire students to write their own versions of stories. "I'm writing my own *virgin* of Red Riding Hood!" one little girl proudly told me during a school visit. Teachers can read aloud fairy tales, invite students to choose one,

"Writing begins with experience itself, with a full, deep experiencing of life in all its colors and textures."
—Jerry Spinelli (2000)

and then write it from a different point of view. For example, how would it feel to be the wicked stepmother in Cinderella? Every story has different sides to tell.

Favorite books help inspire a variety of writing. Children who enjoy the Magic Tree House time-travel stories can write Mary Pope Osborne letters suggesting where to send Jack and Annie next. Also, they can write their own Magic Tree House adventures. All of the Magic Tree House stories involve research. Show students how to do research, using the school library and the Internet. They can keep a written record of research results—just like Annie and Jack.

Older students reading *Maniac Magee* or *Loser* can choose a character in one of the books and examine how he or she handled a situation. Jerry Spinelli's characters face tough decisions, and sometimes they make bad choices. After you discuss "what-ifs," your students can rewrite the scene.

In Cornelia Funke's magical adventure *Inkheart*, a young girl discovers that she can make book characters come to life by reading a book aloud. What book characters would your students like to make real? Which storybook world would they like to visit? Kids can write about what character they would bring to life and into which book they would like to step.

J.K. Rowling, author of Harry Potter, always knew she wanted to become a writer. "To me there is nothing more important than reading, particularly if you want to be a writer. Reading gives you more power and adds a little magic to your life."

In *Nonfiction Matters*, Stephanie Harvey says "Our favorite authors can be our best teachers. We grow to know them through their books, and we learn about writing by reading their work" (1998: 10). Encourage kids to check out their favorite authors' websites. They can watch for new books, see their favorite characters, and write an e-mail.

Feast Your Eyes on a Good Book

Display books face-out on shelves and ledges to give kids a visual feast for the eyes. Kids always gravitate to books that face out over those just showing a spine. A well-stocked classroom includes the following kinds of texts:

- Easy and hard books for boys and girls; an assortment for every interest
- A variety of genres such as picture books, fiction, nonfiction, and poetry
- Favorite authors and illustrators; seasonal and thematic tie-ins
- Non-traditional formats, such as graphic novels, magazines, and comic books
- Award winners, recommended titles; interesting content and good illustrations

Give Kids a Choice

Involve your kids in choosing classroom materials. Invite student volunteers to visit the library every week or two, and get about 30 new books for the class. As a group, discuss the guidelines for picking good books (see above). This enhances their sense of ownership and interest in new resources. When they return, display the new books and talk about them.

Give 30-Second Book Talks

One teacher I met starts every morning with a 30-second book talk. What a great idea! Kids welcome verbal recommendations. Every day, choose any book from your display and talk about it. Say the title, read the blurb on the back cover, and tell about the author. Read the first few lines to give students a sense of the book. If possible, show one or two illustrations. Identify any special features (e.g., awards) and other books by the same person.

After you have modeled several book talks, invite volunteers from around the room to do one. Many students have titles they want to share with the class and benefit from each other's recommendations. The book helps as a prop when facing an audience. Using this approach, students gain valuable experience giving oral presentations.

One time, I asked teachers, "How many days are there in a school year?"

"Too many!" they replied. Joking aside, most districts have nearly 200 teaching days each year. Just think—by giving a 30-second book talk every day, you will recommend nearly 200 books to your students. Book talks get kids excited about reading and writing. Remember to highlight nonfiction titles too.

Use Your Halls and Walls to Teach…

Over the course of many read-alouds, create class charts of author's techniques. Some of the most concrete, accessible strategies are

- Catchy titles
- Voice
- Great leads
- Settings
- Verbs
- Similes

…and Convey Valuable Messages

Find quotations on writing that relate to your lesson. Use quotations from authors that students will recognize. Post them in your room, quote them verbally, print them on handouts, or use them in newsletters. When student writers hear what accomplished writers say about their craft, it makes an impact. Throughout this book, I have provided many quotations from children's authors. See also page 106 for some quotes on Writing (and Editing).

> "Teachers can set up classrooms that encourage kids to live a rich nonfiction life, a life of passion, wonder, and excitement. Inquiry-based classrooms should sing nonfiction. The wall, the halls, the print, the shelves and the furnishings can invite further exploration."
> — Stephanie Harvey, *Nonfiction Matters* (1998: 42)

Writing Tip from Jane Yolen

"I have three pieces of advice for young writers. One: read, read, read! You must read every day, and try to read a wide range of books. Two: write, write, write! Keep a journal, write letters, anything to keep the 'writing muscles' in shape. Three: don't let anyone stop you from writing. Be persistent no matter what 'naysayers' or critical editors have to say about your writing."

Hobbies and Interests

> "The most important thing anybody ever told me was to write what you know."
> —Eric Walters

When your students want writing topics, encourage them to consider their interests. Given the chance, what do they talk about endlessly? What drives them to seek out information? What do they like doing? If they like dance, they might write about that. If they love horses, they might write about that. Kids are keener when they care about the writing subject. Have them explore topics that touch them personally—make it meaningful to their lives.

Topics surface from writer's interests. While some authors create stories of make-believe, others detail events in history, or tell about people in sports. Regardless of the genre, we write best about things that stimulate us. With the use of active verbs, lively headings, and colorful descriptions, nonfiction writing can be as exciting as fiction.

Teachers can share a few of their own interests as a model. Then ask kids to think about their interests – things they enjoy, know about, want to know about – and list them on the computer or in a notebook. Notice this Grade 3 boy's interests:

Gr. 3

Things I like
king Tut
Exploring
Nessi
Castles
Science
Skiing
History
Rockets
Volcanos
Planes
Lost Shipwreks
✓Greek myths

A Grade 4 class in King City prepared for the annual public speaking contest at their school. Their teacher said to write about things they knew, liked, and wanted to learn more about. Students could choose their topic based on the following criteria:

- Do you enjoy it?
- Do you know a lot about it?
- Could you explain it to others?
- Do you want to learn more about it?

Then they were to write as much as possible about it. After exhausting all prior knowledge about their topic, they researched for more information in the school library, on the Internet, and from other sources. One boy chose to write about his passion—Lego. Later, he represented the class with these words:

Savage pirates! Brave knights! Blasting cannon balls! If you've grown up in the last 45 years chances are you've had all kinds of exciting adventures with Lego.

With Lego, anything is possible. Two eight-studded plastic bricks can be joined in twenty-four different ways. Six can be joined in over a hundred million ways! Add other pieces, different colors and sizes, gears, tiny human figures and the inventions are endless.

Lego comes in twelve colors. From magnets to capes and hats to wigs, you can customize your man, woman or even robot with Lego accessories.

Lego has grown from a little shop in Denmark to international sales. A Danish man named Ole Kirk Christiansen invented this toy. As a child, Ole carved whistles and little human figures. One day he started carving building blocks. People bought so many that Ole started producing the blocks full time. He combined two Danish words *"leg godt"* (meaning "play well") and got the name Lego.

Ole had high standards. He wanted his toys to be sturdy and long-lasting. In 1958, Lego produced plastic bricks in its current stud-and-tube design. It proved so popular that Lego created Duplo for toddlers. Then came Lego Technic for older kids.

Some day I want to visit Legoland, a theme park in Denmark. It has hundreds of exhibits all made from Lego. Visitors can see replicas, ride a Merry-Lego-Round and make their own Lego creations.

If you can't go to Denmark, why not visit my house? The first thing I'd show you is my Lego Lab. It's a large area in our basement. I call it a lab because I do a lot of tinkering and inventing there.

While we were studying the Middle Ages in school, I invented a Medieval tower. During the O.J. Simpson trial, I built a courtroom with a judge and two people for the jury. Res-Q Headquarters is my favorite Lego creation. I built the whole thing myself. It's in the shape of an L and took a month to build.

There are always new possi-build-ities for you to try. Just imagine! Maybe someday we could build an Air bus, a replica of the Titanic, or the CN Tower. Together we can take Lego to all new heights.

This speech is fun to read. The writer's enthusiasm for his topic made research and writing enjoyable. In the end, he came second schoolwide in the public speaking contest.

Nature

When I was 18, I worked at the Columbia Icefield in Jasper National Park. There, experienced driver-guides take passengers on a tour of the Athabaska Glacier. At the turn-around point, people can step out onto the large ice mass and peer down deep crevasses in the rock. I loved everything about this Rocky Mountain adventure—living within some of the most spectacular scenery in Western Canada, hiking into high alpine meadows, and especially meeting wildlife in its natural habitat. On any given day, we saw big bull elk, mountain goats, deer, and moose. One evening a grizzly bear visited our staff camp. That was an experience to write home about!

Nature inspires many writers. Jean Craighead George, for example, has written more than 100 books for children, including her novels *Julie of the Wolves* and *My Side of the Mountain*. She, like many writers, gets ideas from nature. Teachers can read aloud books based on nature and offer kids an opportunity to write nature poems, stories, and nonfiction.

For more on Visual Presentation, see Chapter 7.

Renowned wildlife artist Robert Bateman demonstrates reader-friendly non-fiction writing in *Backyard Birds*. This book offers profiles of the birds that nature-lovers might see in their community. Chock-full of rich language, it is an exceptional example of how to present expository writing in an interesting and informative way. Beginning with the title (*Backyard Birds*), Introduction ("Birth of a Birder"), and other headings, Bateman uses alliteration to attract his audience. A typical spread includes one large illustration, a few paragraphs of first-person text, and captions and sidebars about each featured bird. Not only is the simple text well-organized and easy to follow, but Bateman's narrative also evokes the senses. To describe Great Horned Owls, for example, he says, "You may hear their loud 'hoo-hoo-hoo' from the deep woods." And he explains the Great Blue Heron's hunting skills with this simile: "Seeing something, it snaps its neck like a whip—"

Animal watching is a wonderful activity for children and adults to share. In 2010, my husband's mapping job led us to a conference in Hawaii. One afternoon, we went whale-watching off the coast of Maui. It was peak season and we experienced all sorts of whale activity up close. I will always remember the thrill of seeing these gentle giants lift their tails to dive and hearing the thunderous *splash!* moments later. We watched a mother teaching her calf how to breach and babies jumping for joy, happy to be alive.

Jane Yolen has written more than 300 books, many inspired by nature. *Owl Moon* depicts the sights, sounds, and feelings of a father and daughter who are owl-watching on a cold winter night. She dedicates this picture book to her husband, who took all of their children owling. On her website she describes *Owl Moon* as her "best known work," but she also wrote a book of poems called *Bird Watch*. Yolen belongs to a family of bird watchers. She watched her husband David (the original Pa from *Owl Moon*) interact with birds, children, and other birders. Chances are, your students have animal-watching experiences to share and write about.

Others writers inspired by nature:

Farley Mowat—Having an owl as a childhood pet inspired *Owls in the Family*.

Gary Paulsen—His experiences in the north woods inspired *Woodsong*.

Dr. Phil Gates—How nature inspired today's engineering and technology in *Nature Got There First*

Jan Thornhill—A worldwide tour in *The Wildlife ABC & 123: A Nature Alphabet & Counting Book*

Margriet Ruurs—Awe-inspiring scenes and sentences about life in *In My Backyard*.

Diane Swanson—Fascinating behaviors of owls inspired *Welcome to the World of Owls*.

Jan Brett—Beautiful greens of spring and summer inspired *The Umbrella*.

Likewise, nature has inspired author Kenneth Oppel. In *Silverwing*, he bases all of his characters on real species of bats. Once Oppel started reading about bats, he realized how fascinating they were. He was interested in the idea of a migration. Then he wondered: What would happen if a young bat got lost on his first migration; how would he find his way? Would he have some kind of map? Would someone help him? He invented the notion of sound maps sung from one bat to another and of the echo chamber, but they don't seem too farfetched.

Lori Baskin, an outstanding Grade 5 language arts teacher, had her class publish poetry anthologies. First, she asked everyone to read all kinds of poems and provided each student with a one-page Poetry Reading Log to fill in. As they read, kids recorded the book, poem title, and poet (see template on page 38).

SOURCE (BOOK)	Page #	POEM TITLE	POET
The Cremation of Sam McGee	Whole book	The Cremation of Sam McGee	Robert W. Service
The Shooting of Dan McGrew	" "	The Shooting of Dan McGrew	" "
Dirty Dog Boogie	10	I Hate Poetry	Loris Lesynski
"	"	6	Dirty Dog Boogie	=
"	"	8	SOS	"	"

Each student wrote and illustrated 25 kinds of poems, organized them into a table of contents, designed covers, and published the poems into booklets. Many parents consider these booklets family treasures.

Michelle, inspired by nature, wrote this definition poem:

> Rain is…
> Rain is the tears of Heaven
> Rain is the quenching of Mother Nature's parched throat
> Rain is the cleansing of nature's soul
> Rain is the new seeds of life
> Rain is a joy for farmers in their fields
> Rain is the sustenance for daily needs
> Rain is a part of a never ending cycle that we call life.

When writing poetry, having a thesaurus and rhyming dictionary nearby helps. They are terrific resources to keep in the classroom and to recommend for use at home.

My son Cory entitled his anthology "Piles of Poems"—a boyish attempt at alliteration. Inspired by the sights and sounds of nature at our summer cottage in northern Ontario, here is an excerpt from his collection:

INVITATION

Come up to my cottage tree fort
It's the best of its sort.
You'll hear water lapping
And woodpeckers tapping.
You'll get a great view
Of the water so blue.
You can see the cottage eaves
And lots of green leaves.
As you hear voices ringing
Birds are merrily singing.

Dreams

Kids often say that one of their favorite books is *The BFG* by Roald Dahl. In this story, a Big Friendly Giant catches good dreams and blows them into the bedrooms of children. When he catches a nightmare, he bottles it forever. The BFG struggles with grammar until a little girl named Sophie teaches him how to speak and write properly.

Occasionally dreams stir up writing ideas. Teachers can use *The BFG* as a springboard to discussing dreams. While some kids can remember what they dreamed the night before and write about it, most prefer telling dreams of the future.

Whenever I do student workshops, I try to build on the natural link between spoken and written language. Often I'll pose this question: "What do you want to be when you grow up?" Kids have interesting thoughts on this. Most delight in telling their dream jobs:

"A veterinarian"
"Brain surgeon"
"Hockey player"

With each response, I'll ask "Why?" (my never-ending prompt for details!). Their replies vary widely and fascinate me. After several students reveal what they want to be and give supporting details, I invite them to write about it. A Grade 4 boy's story went like this:

I'm curious. When I grow up, I want to be a detective, a scientist or a police officer. Once I hear something interesting I always want to know more. I love learning and I ask a lot of questions, such as:
1. Do carnivores get scurvy?
2. Do magnets work in water?

Sometimes, one response leads to other topics of inquiry, as the example shows. Stephanie Harvey says questions of substance—like *Do carnivores get scurvy?* Or *Do magnets works in water?*—"emerge from the curiosity of a learner who knows enough about the topic to ask a thoughtful question" (1998: 27).

Indulge inquisitiveness. Encourage kids who question to research and conduct experiments for more information. In my workshops, I urge kids to be brave and take risks. Remember: every question you get indicates interest. Welcome it!

After a similar discussion about dream jobs with an older group, a Grade 7 student wrote:

I hope to become a Lego Master Builder. Master Builders are the people that design and build the massive Lego structures you see outside toy stores. It is their job to build the huge Lego displays for museums all around the world.

I researched Master Builders online. One worked as a mail sorter, and as a way of taking his mind off things, he played with Lego. Eventually Lego headquarters found out about him and contracted him to do work. Another man worked in a pastry shop until he decided to chance occupations. Many Master Builders have backgrounds in CAD (computer-aided design). Others, like the pastry shop man have training in set design. All, however, have extraordinary imaginations and are highly innovative.

Authentic, meaty writing arises from dreams of the future. And kids go to great lengths to answer questions that compel them.

Equally, kids enjoy talking about places they'd like to go someday. I'll ask them, "If you could travel anywhere in the world, where would it be? Why?" Often kids will name their country of origin. To me, that's like hitting the jackpot. It's a clue that they have many more stories to tell—and write about. Value their diversity. Remind them that they all bring unique perspectives to the table.

Recently, Grade 4 student Durga moved to Canada and began learning English. She starts her story like this:

> I would go to Sri Lanka to see my grandparents. And they would say, "How beautiful you look!"

You can hear the joyfulness in Durga's voice. Already she can describe the event, even though it is a dream of the future. And listen to her authenticity! I'd like to hear more of Durga's story.

Michelle, in Grade 5, wrote the striking poem below, based on her dreams.

Invitation

Have you ever yearned to be some place
Where you didn't have a care?
Just close your eyes and open your mind
And your thoughts will take you there.
A place where birds whistle melodies, all the morning long
And all night there's celebrations, with lots of dance and song.
Where bushes and shrubs grow gumdrops, and, if you please,
Lollipops and candy bars are growing from the trees.
Where all the streets are paved with gold, and the grass the brightest green,
And everyone had equal rights, there is no King or Queen.
But alas, in the end, this is just my fantasy,
And we each have our dreams of how the world should be.

This is a beautiful example of how all the writing traits work together: ideas, organization, word choice, voice, fluency, and conventions.

Lucy Maud Montgomery remains one of Canada's most cherished writers. Despite living in a time when women stayed home to raise children, Maud dreamed of becoming an author. She had many jobs—teaching, working for a newspaper, running the local post office—on the way to her dream, ultimately writing 24 books, 530 short stories, and 500 poems in her career. In 1905, Maud started writing her first novel, a story about a lively redhead named Anne. After many rejections, *Anne of Green Gables* was published in 1908 and became an instant bestseller.

Friendships and Families

Friends and families inspire all kinds of writing. Some are celebratory, others are sad, while still others are observations. Kids can write something special about a friend, family member, sibling relationship, or family pet.

Robert Munsch wrote a serious story called *Lighthouse – A Story of Remembrance*. In this book, Sarah and her father set off in the dark, on a special journey in honor of her grandpa. Whenever we discuss that story, I say to kids, "Describe one memory you have of someone in your family." They all have tales to tell.

Award winner Barbara Reid bases *The Party* on a big family celebration. As an only child, she adored the wild games that she and her cousins would play while the adults were busy talking and eating. In Frieda Wishinsky's *Please, Louise!* Jake wishes his little sister would leave, but Louise wants to be as close to him as she can. Jane Yolen's *Owl Moon* depicts the special companionship of a young child and her father. In Karen Ackerman's *Song and Dance Man*, the children are delighted with their grandfather's antics and his tales of long ago when he was young, dancing on the vaudeville stage.

When kids look on times of their life—like elementary school and summer camp—often thoughts of their friends stick out the most. The joys and pitfalls of friendship inspire many of the best books for kids. Students, too, can write stories based on friendships. These prompts may give them writing ideas:

- Your best friend tells you a secret. Describe the conversation.
- The craziest experience you've ever shared with your friends.
- You are partners with your friend in a science project. She is doing absolutely no work. How do you approach her about it?
- Describe meeting your best friend in the world.

Also, encourage kids to share these writings with a friend after they write them. If they write from the heart, chances are their friends will be proud. Sophie (Grade 5, age 10) wrote this acrostic poem about her best friend Charlotte:

See also page 31 for Memories as sources for writing.

More books about friends and family:
Little Women by Louisa May Alcott
Tales of a Fourth Grade Nothing by Judy Blume
Henry Huggins by Beverly Cleary
Matilda by Roald Dahl
Because of Winn Dixie by Kate DiCamillo
The Mother-Daughter Book Club by Heather Vogel Frederick
Anne of Green Gables by Lucy Maud Montgomery
The All-New Amelia by Marissa Moss

Caring and always ready to
Help those in need
Active and sporty
Really good at french
Loves her sister
Optimistic at all times
The best big sister
Talkative and spunky
Everyone's friend

Memories

"I get my ideas from remembering what it was like being a kid," explained Paulette Bourgeois, creator of Franklin the turtle, in an interview. Memories evoke writing ideas for many children's authors. Jane Barclay offers a meaningful introduction to remembrance in *Proud as a Peacock, Brave as a Lion*. This gentle, lyrical story depicts a grandpa answering his grandson's questions about serving in the war. In *The Memory String* by Eve Bunting, a girl clings to memories while grieving for her mother and feeling unable to accept her stepmother. Lois Lowry wrote *The Giver*, a science-fiction novel set in the future. It follows a boy named Jonas through his twelfth year of life. He becomes Receiver of Memory because of his unusual Capacity to See-Beyond his world: violence, sadness, and loss; as well as love, beauty, joy, adventure, animals, and family.

What's Your Earliest Memory?

A food fight stirs cultural sensitivity and conflict resolution in *The Sandwich Swap*, a children's book launched in 2010 at the United Nations Bookshop. Queen Rania of Jordan co-authored the book, basing it on her early memories of tasting a classmate's peanut butter sandwich.

Now and then, I tell students about one of my first memories: the time Pierre, our French poodle, ate a pound of butter from a grocery bag in our car. Then I ask them to describe their early memories. Most kids remember their first pet. Students can write about a beloved cat, dog, or gerbil. They can make their story humorous, sad, or nostalgic. Encourage writers to pick a specific incident that stands out in their minds. They may decide to use dialogue or to tell the story from the pet's perspective.

Kids can re-create their memories using taste, touch, smell, sight, and sound. Teachers can offer the following prompt: *I remember...*

Manny, age 12, writes, "I actually remember learning to read. The first word I read was CAT. I remember that reading came easily for me. I also remember reading Curious George over and over again because we couldn't afford new books."

Manny's response leads to another great question for every student: What's Your Earliest Memory of Reading? Abby, age 13, writes, "My parents bought me books every time we went to the grocery store, and then took turns reading them to me. When I was four, our neighbors gave me a pile of old textbooks their kids no longer needed. I still have one of them. We went to lots of garage sales on weekends, and I could always count on a book or comic. I don't remember my parents reading for themselves that much... just magazines and the farmer's almanac, but they encouraged me to enjoy books."

Memoirs by beloved children's authors:
Moon and I by Betsy Byars
A Girl from Yamhill: A Memoir by Beverly Cleary
Boy: Tales of Childhood by Roald Dahl
Looking Back: A Book of Memories by Lois Lowry
Never Cry Wolf: Amazing True Story of Life Among Arctic Wolves by Farley Mowat
Woodsong by Gary Paulsen
When I Was Young in the Mountains by Cynthia Rylant
Knots in My Yo-Yo String: The Autobiography of a Kid by Jerry Spinelli

Thoughts and Feelings

At the Opening Ceremony of the 2010 Olympic Winter Games, poet Shane Koyczan burst onto the world stage with his powerful performance of "We Are More." His presentation became a Twitter sensation and the talk of media forums around the world. I saw it mentioned on blog after blog. Many people described it as the most moving moment of the ceremonies.

Koyczan said that, when officials asked him to participate in the opening ceremonies with his poem, he hesitated for a moment. But then he remembered something his grandmother said: "Once you say 'no' to an opportunity, it's gone and so are all the opportunities that could have come with it." (Brown, 2010)

"We Are More" shows Koyczan's feelings for Canada. His message reminds me how feelings—of love, joy, anger, sadness, and fear—trigger writing ideas. Moreover, his grandmother's message testifies to the rewards of risk and adventure. Ask students, "What the hardest thing you've ever faced? What has bothered you, made you sad, or—on the other hand—excited you?" This will encourage thoughtful discussion and writing ideas.

Strong feelings make a poem powerful. But Shane Koyczan's story begins before the Winter Olympics. In 2008, he wrote a YA novel in verse called *Stickboy* in which he takes on another fear—bullying. The title refers to the "sticks and stones" proverb and the narrator's feelings when classmates bully him. Koyczan based *Stickboy* on his childhood.

Feelings of fear prove a popular theme in young children's books too. Take *Scaredy Squirrel* by Mélanie Watt, one of School Library Journal's Top 100 Picture Books. Scaredy Squirrel never leaves his nut tree. Then one day, he leaps into the unknown, and discovers something uplifting…

The media and warnings everywhere influenced Mélanie Watt. She wanted to write about a neurotic character who overanalyzes and focuses on the risks, so much that he forgets to live his life. Watt explains,

> For a long time I wanted to write a book about fearing the unknown. I grew up in an overly cautious family. I set my mind on exploring this subject and expressing how fear stops us from discovering our talents and capabilities. A squirrel seemed to be the perfect vehicle for this and the nut tree was a good metaphor to start with. The humoristic approach and exaggeration brought this story together. (Watt, 2009)

Often other people's writing looks like it came easily to them. The reality is that good writing takes great effort. My son is an avid reader, but has always struggled with getting writing ideas. Once when he needed inspiration for a free verse poem, he burst into the kitchen where I was working. "Some people think writing poetry is easy!" he protested. "Like you just pull words out of a hat, line them up, and voilà! You have a poem."

"Write that down," I said calmly.

"What?" he stopped.

"Write what you just said!" I repeated.

By expressing his feelings of frustration verbally, he came up with the following poem:

Metrophobia*
Some people say
That writing poetry is easy
You just pull words out of a hat
Align them a certain way
And voilà! You have a poem.
Not so.
You have to tinker with adjectives

Battle with syllable counts
Search for rhyming words
Tap out rhythms
Juggle your thoughts
Fiddle with your feelings
And hope in the end
You've said something meaningful.

* Metrophobia refers to an abnormal and persistent fear of poetry.

I love the way this poem came together. Verbs like *tinker, battle, search, tap, juggle, fiddle,* and *hope* give energy to the piece. Cory's use of alliteration—for example: *some people say, fiddle with your feelings*—enhances the sound. He grasps the ideas of organization and fluency. And you can't miss his voice.

Imagination

Several years ago, I visited a school in London, Ontario. A student escorted me to the library, which was bursting with books and kids conferring about their stories. The teacher-librarian welcomed me into her hub of activity. Writing strategies, kids' work, and popular author websites covered the walls. Many students participated in the Forest of Reading® program, for which they read a list of books and voted on their top picks.

Talking about good authors proved easy at this school. A buzz filled the room, as kids enthusiastically named which writers they like best, and why. One animated Grade 7 girl blurted, "Bill Richardson! *After Hamelin*—hands down, best book I ever read." What a response!

Truly, *After Hamelin* is a joy in language, full of songs, rhymes, poems, skipping chants, and incantations. The author uses inventive wordplay and his imagination. In this wonderfully woven tale, Penelope journeys into a dangerous dream world to save her friends from the evil Pied Piper. She remembers and recounts this story at age 101. As she writes about her adventure, she begins to sound feisty again, realizing that she can still do good in the world. Imagination doesn't end at the last pages for some. Many readers want to write a tale of their own.

Mary Pope Osborne has written more than 42 books in the *Magic Tree House* series. She spent a year figuring out how Jack and Anne would get back in time. She tried magic whistles, a magic cellar, a magic museum, a magic artist's studio... but none of these ideas worked. One day, on a walk in the country, she saw a kid's treehouse. By nightfall, she decided that the brother and sister would travel in a magic treehouse. Sometimes the simplest ideas prove the hardest to come up with!

Do you have a future fantasy author in your class? Christopher Paolini, the author of *Eragon*, was only 15 when he began writing this acclaimed novel. Help start your students on their fantasy story by asking them these five questions:

1. What is the name of your fantasy world?
2. Name three things you would notice there.
3. What is the name of your main character?
4. What special traits and magical powers does your character have?
5. What unusual event begins your story?

While authors like Bill Richardson and Christopher Paolini both enjoy the world of imagination, not everybody can write about dangerous dream worlds and magical powers. Not everybody likes to pretend. Many of us prefer the "real world" of current events, and would rather use our imaginations to write interesting nonfiction.

Other Sources of Writing Ideas:
- Pictures
- Songs
- Current Events, Real Life, Unexpected Events
- TV and Movies
- Radio and Computers
- Places We Go

Best-selling author Judy Blume never seems to run out of great writing ideas. She says that they come from everywhere—her life; everything she sees, hears, and reads; and especially from her imagination. To her, stories mix reality and imagination. She encourages students to take the time to daydream and let their imaginations run wild. If she can get a good first sentence, she can usually write a story to go with it. See if that works for your students! Judy Blume spent her childhood in New Jersey, making up stories in her head. She has written more than 20 books, including her hilarious Fudge series. In *Tales of a Fourth Grade Nothing*, Fudge is based on her son Larry when he was a toddler.

Ideas pop up at any moment. Exploring how authors get their ideas can start creative juices flowing. To encourage student writing, include in your tool kit as many of the different techniques described in the preceding pages as it will hold.

Now You've Got the Idea…What Next?

Add Interesting Details

Good writing features interesting details. Capturing an event through descriptive writing involves paying attention to the details. Regular writing practice helps kids become more observant and confident. Once children decide on an idea to write about, these prompts help them bring details to the surface:

- Tell what's happening around you—*who, what, when, where, how,* and *why.*
- Be specific. For example, instead of tree, say what kind of tree.
- Concentrate on what happens. Answer these questions:
  - What do you see? Hear? Smell? Taste?
  - How does the place feel: temperature? textures?
  - How do you feel: excited? scared? happy? sad?
  - What are you thinking?

I use oral storytelling to show students how details create a picture in the listener/reader's mind. We begin by looking at a children's book such as *Franklin in the Dark*. In that story, Franklin the turtle is afraid of the dark and too scared to go in his shell. Then I relate something true from my life, like my fear of the dark. I tell about the night I went downstairs alone and heard strange noises. I saw a bird flying around in our basement!

Writing Tip from Phyllis Reynolds Naylor
(author of *Shiloh*)

"Once I have the idea for a story. I start collecting all kinds of helpful information and storing it in three-ring notebooks. For example, I may see a picture of a man in a magazine and say, 'That's exactly what the father in my book looks like!'... I save everything that will help—maps, articles, hand-jotted notes, bits of dialogue from conversations that I overhear."

Ask Open-Ended Questions

Once kids have a general picture in their minds, I invite anyone to ask questions beginning with *Who? What? Where? Why? When?* and *How?* Open-ended questions give a person scope for details and require a response. Skimpy storytellers cannot shrug and answer with a simple "yes" or "no":

> "How big was the bird?" someone might ask.
> "I'd say as big as a house, but I felt too afraid to look."
> "How did it get there?"
> "He came through the chimney."

Their questions help me add details to draw a more effective image.

After my story, kids want to tell about their fears of the dark. Some have many details. Others don't. Throughout the year, students can prompt each other with open-ended questions. Soon children realize that they all have stories to tell. Use clue words to help them elaborate: who, what, where, when, why, and how. By asking good questions, they help one another to create more vivid pictures in people's minds.

Let Them Talk

Robert Munsch has hundreds of story ideas. But sometimes he has trouble writing the words. He says, "We all learn to talk before we learn to write. It helps to say stories out loud." The popular storyteller makes sense—oral language helps writing skills to develop. The day my son was born, my grandma advised, "Talk to him. Talk to him all the time, and soon he will learn words too."

Elementary students are still learning to talk—not "baby talk" anymore, but "bigger" words. (Some teachers like to say "juicy" words.) From their expanding experiences, children begin using more explicit and diverse vocabulary. We know that oral language forms the basis for reading and writing skills, so kids need to engage in activities that encourage talking. Give them opportunities to strengthen their oral language skills: interaction with peers and adults, both one-on-one and in groups. They need to engage in conversations. They need to listen and respond to stories. These activities develop their vocabulary. This, by extension, will help them with writing.

Several years ago, my husband and I visited Kinkaku-Ji (Temple of the Golden Pavilion) in Kyoto, Japan. Dozens of eyes grew wide when a group of Japanese high-school students spotted us. "Hel-lo," they said shyly, wanting to practice their English. My husband agreed to let them interview him. A few minutes later, their teacher appeared. "Thank you for helping our students. Yesterday they had a Japanese language test. They must do well to leave school and go out into the world."

This reminds me of a standard literacy test, I thought, one to establish that students have reached a mature level of language. Up until students have reached that level, consider your students still *learning* to talk. As kids learn to talk, they learn to be good writers, too.

Some people need to talk through their ideas before writing about them. We saw this in our son from an early age. He enjoys reading, but seemed to freeze up with every writing assignment. Whenever possible, I would sit at the kitchen table and have him verbalize his thoughts before writing about them. He needed to say his ideas before he could commit them to writing. Being able to talk it through gave him a surge of confidence. And even though I usually felt unfamiliar with his subject matter, this social interaction helped him produce.

Many authors join writer's groups for this social component. Talking through their ideas helps them become successful, engaged writers. I suggest a similar approach in the classroom. Form small writers groups. Encourage kids to talk about their ideas, discuss their writing, offer each other support, and work together on strategies.

Battling Writer's Block

Most days writers hit a wall of some kind. Being stuck is one of the most frustrating experiences a writer can face. When Victor Hugo couldn't write *Les Miserables*, he *felt* miserable—from writer's block. His cure? He stripped naked for hours, during which time he would only have access to a pen and paper. That way, he could do little else but write. (*Mental Floss*)

Countless reasons explain writer's block: fear, anxiety, a life change, the beginning of a project…

In writing this book, I always tried to end my day (or morning or evening) when I was doing well. If I knew how to finish a section, I looked forward to returning. Explain to students that stopping and starting on a high note boosts self-confidence and motivation.

Writing Tip from Ernest Hemingway

"The best way is always to stop when you are doing good and when you know what will happen next. If you do that every day…you will never be stuck." — from *A Moveable Feast* by Ernest Hemingway

Roald Dahl comments:

"I never come back to a blank page; I always finish about halfway through. Hemingway taught me the finest trick: "When you are going good, stop writing…walk away…you can't wait to get back because know what you want to say next." — from *The Roald Dahl Treasury* by Roald Dahl

---

If your students struggle with writer's block, they're in good company. Some of our greatest writers have battled the block. But all of them found ways to deal with it, and we need to help kids find strategies that work for them. Author Kenneth Oppel (*Sunwing, Silverwing, Firewing* and *Darkwing*) offers excellent insight on his website:

> When most people talk about writer's block, they mean a longish period of weeks or months or even years! But I think every writer faces micro versions of block throughout each working day. Writing, like life, involves so many different options and possibilities that it's often paralyzing. When I get stuck, I usually do one of two things. One, I jump forwards, to a part of the story where I know what happens. Two, I go backwards and rethink what I've already written. Because sometimes when you get stuck, it means you've left unfinished work behind you.

Kenneth Oppel writes mainly fiction and picture books. His technique of "jumping forward" and "going backwards" works for nonfiction writers too. I have used that strategy in writing this book, and it works to keep up the momentum. For me, a number of strategies help beat writer's block. Sometimes I need to stretch—get up and move around. Other times, I go out for a brisk walk. Often, I talk with others to help problem-solve.

Almost anything can cause the feelings of fear and frustration in writer's block. Luckily, many ways exist to deal with it. Encouraging students to try something new becomes the first step toward writing again. Throughout this book, you'll find Block Buster tips for students who feel stuck.

"Ideas are the cheapest part of the writing. They are free. The hard part is what you do with ideas you've gathered."

— Jane Yolen

Block Buster: Brainstorm

Brainstorming brings writing ideas. Pick a topic that you're interested in. Then write down every related word that comes to mind. For example, if your topic is dogs, write down *leashes, dog food, ball, bones, collar, Frisbee, walking, pet,* and *friend*. Keep brainstorming on your topic and a story idea will come.

Poetry Reading Log

for_____

Title of Book	Page Number	Title of Poem	Poet

Pembroke Publishers © 2010 *How Bullets Saved My Life* by Judy Green ISBN 978-1-55138-255-5

2

Organization

> *We honor students' individual learning styles by modeling the entire spectrum of organizational strategies, encouraging them to practice each a few times, and finally allowing them to select the ones that best fit their needs.*
> —Stephanie Harvey, *Nonfiction Matters* (1998: 144)

Organization involves the internal structure of a piece of writing, the logical and sometimes intriguing pattern of ideas. Organized ideas help a reader move through a piece of writing in a meaningful way. Encourage kids to keep these things in mind as they write:

- Does your lead "hook" the reader?
- Is your writing easy to follow?
- Does it make sense?
- Do you stay on topic?
- Is your conclusion satisfying?

Organization means deciding on what to include and arranging things in an order that makes sense. That involves deciding where or how to begin and end. Teach kids how to create powerful beginnings, connect details to the main idea, and conclude in a satisfying way, so that they become well-organized writers. Graphic organizers can help students brainstorm important details. Picture books show different ways that authors organize their ideas.

Writing a Strong Lead

When I grew up, my mom took me to Story Hour at the public library every Saturday morning. Miss Brown, the children's librarian, read aloud to us. My favorite book was *The Story about Ping* by Marjorie Flack. I can still remember how it started: "Once upon a time there was a beautiful young duck named Ping… He lived on a boat with two wise eyes on the Yangtze river."

More recently, I did a writing workshop with Grade 8 students. Their teacher asked, "What ways can we start stories besides 'Once upon a time'?" For sure, a strong lead—the opening sentence or paragraph—matters because it captures the reader's interest. Everyone wants to follow a good lead.

My recommendation? Study how experienced writers start. Every time you read to students—picture books, nonfiction, fiction—come back to the beginning and examine *how* the author started that story. Show kids ways to grab their reader's attention. Strong openings make good first impressions and hook the reader.

When you read a good lead, you know it. Carol Matas, for example, begins her historical fiction novel *Jesper* like this:

> I am to be executed. It will be soon. The Nazis are getting desperate, and the more desperate they get, the meaner they get.

Those first few sentences prompted a Grade 6 boy to write this in his Reading Response Journal:

> I felt shocked when I first read that. What a powerful opening line! I have never read such a strong beginning. I wanted to read on. I felt intrigued to find out more background information.

Teachers can use picture books at all grade levels to demonstrate leads. I love the beginning of *The True Story of the 3 Little Pigs!* (by A. Wolf):

> Everybody knows the story of the Three Little Pigs. Or at least they think they do. But I'll let you in on a secret…

See how Jon Scieszka uses intrigue to catch our attention?

You can teach many ways to create strong beginnings. Some teachers even post a chart entitled Good Leads by Good Authors so that students have access to examples all year long. As the year progresses, add more from your reading. This chart shows good leads in fiction for older students:

GOOD LEADS BY GOOD AUTHORS

Book	Author	Lead
Death In the Air	*Shane Peacock*	*What is it like to see a man die right before your eyes?*
Holes	*Louis Sachar*	*There is no lake at Camp Green Lake.*
Camp X	*Eric Walters*	*A twig snapped under my feet and I froze at the sound.*

As well, invite students to look at leads from their own books. Research the ones in your class and school library. Consider a variety of genres, including picture books, short stories, novels, and nonfiction. Each student should be able to find several examples. Read and discuss them together. Choose first lines that invite an immediate response.

Experienced writers usually choose their leads from a variety of categories. When your students need ways to start, this list might help.

Ten Top Ways to Start Stories

1. Character's Name

Introduce a person or person-like object.

> "Grace was a girl who loved stories." *Amazing Grace* by Mary Hoffman
> "Sophie couldn't sleep. A brilliant moonbeam was slanting through a gap in the curtains." *The BFG* by Roald Dahl
> "Samuel woke up really hungry." *More Pies!* by Robert Munsch

Other picture books with great beginnings include
How I Became a Pirate by Melinda Long and David Shannon
The Library by Sarah Stewart
The Polar Express by Chris Van Allsburg
Hey Little Ant by Phillip and Hannah Hoose
Shrek by William Steig

2. Question

Present a puzzle or mystery for the reader to ponder.

> "How does one describe Artemis Fowl? Various psychiatrists have tried and failed." *Artemis Fowl* by Eoin Colfer
> "Where's Papa going with that ax?" *Charlotte's Web* by E.B. White
> "What is it like to see a man die right before your eyes?" *Death in the Air* (The Boy Sherlock Holmes, His 2nd Case) by Shane Peacock

3. Sound

A tried and true device to capture the reader's attention.

> "Piiiiinnnggg! The bell rang out as I opened the door to the general store." *The Bully Boys* by Eric Walters
> "Life was going along okay when my mother and father dropped the news. *Bam!* Just like that." *Superfudge* by Judy Blume

4. Powerful Emotion

Reveal the writer or main character's true self.

> "The day she was born was the happiest day in her parents' lives." *Chrysanthemum* by Kevin Henkes
> "It was almost December, and Jonas was beginning to be frightened." *The Giver* by Lois Lowry
> "A twig snapped under my feet and I froze at the sound." *Camp X* by Eric Walters

5. Unusual Image

Use this powerful tool to create a dramatic scene.

> "My father's loft was as silent as a mortuary and as dark as the inside of a coffin – except for the glow from his study." *Out of the Cold* by Norah McClintock
> "The storm boiled above the Indian Ocean, a dark, bristling wall of cloud, blocking our passage west." *Skybreaker* by Kenneth Oppel

6. Clear Statement

The writer gives a key piece of information to develop.

> "Louise never left her brother Jake alone." *Please, Louise!* by Frieda Wishinsky
> "Lilly loved school." *Lilly's Purple Plastic Purse* by Kevin Henkes
> "When Joseph was a baby, his grandfather made him a wonderful blanket…" *Something from Nothing"* by Phoebe Gilman
> "Mama taught me to lie." *How It Happened in Peach Hill* by Marthe Jocelyn

7. Setting

The writer describes the place, and sometimes the time of a story.

> "It was late one winter night, long past my bedtime, when Pa and I went owling." *Owl Moon* by Jane Yolen
> "The Lupine lady lives in a small house overlooking the sea. In between the rocks around her house grow blue and purple and rose-colored flowers." *Miss Rumphius* by Barbara Cooney
> "Laura sat under the oak tree in their small back yard." *The Memory String* by Eve Bunting

"In a hole in the ground there lived a hobbit." *The Hobbit* J.R.R. Tolkien
"Sailing towards dawn, and I was perched atop the crow's nest, being the ship's eyes. We were two nights out of Sydney…" *Airborn* by Kenneth Oppel

8. Flashback

The author takes us back to an earlier time. This technique helps us understand more fully the present situation. Flashbacks help capture a reader's attention. I recommend that young writers try them at the beginning of a story, but some authors use them throughout. Since the flashback technique involves action and dialogue, it works well in adventure stories.

> "I looked at the long dirt road that crawled across the plains, remembering the morning that Mama had died, cruel and sunny. They had come for her in a wagon and taken her away." *Sarah, Plain and Tall* by Patricia MacLachlan

Suggested Topics for Flashbacks
- A day I'll always remember
- A big mistake
- Experience pays off
- I learned the hard way

9. Quotation

Write the words of a real person or an invented character.

> "'Mother?' There was no reply." *Gathering Blue* by Lois Lowry
> "Take my word for it, Bruno—you're not going to like him." *Something Fishy at Macdonald Hall* by Gordon Korman
> "Somebody must have told them suckers I was coming." *Fallen Angels* by Walter Dean Myers

10. First-person

A story narrated by only one character that explicitly refers to him- or herself as "I." This allows the reader or audience to see only the narrator's point of view.

> "I went to sleep with gum in my mouth and now there's gum in my hair…" *Alexander and the Terrible, Horrible, No Good, Very Bad Day* by Judith Viorst
> "I blame it all on *The Hobbit*. That, and my supportive home life." *Alice, I Think* by Susan Juby
> "I was thirteen the first time I saw a police officer up close." *Schooled* by Gordon Korman

---

Block Buster: Begin in the Middle

Start writing wherever you like. Begin in the middle, and leave the introduction or first section until later. Some writers routinely save the introduction until they have a better feel for the piece.

Writing Nonfiction Leads

"Where will you find 'blackheads,' 'Chin wigs,' 'roasted dormice' and 'radishes' in an index? In a *Horrible Histories* book, of course!" So begins *Awesome Egyptians* by Terry Deary and Peter Hepplewhite. That opener certainly gets everyone's attention. Teachers can use nonfiction books to demonstrate good beginnings in nonfiction writing.

Seven Sure-Fire Formulas to Begin Nonfiction Writing

1. Ask a question or series of questions, and then state your intention to provide answers. Rhetorical questions get the reader to think about your subject.

> Want to make super-cool jewelry without breaking the bank? How about spending a little time instead of a lot of money?
> —*Junk Drawer Jewelry* by Rachel Di Salle and Ellen Warwick

2. Quote from a book, a teacher, or an authority.

> John McCrae's "In Flanders Fields" is called the most popular poem of the First World War (1914-1918).
> —*Remembering John McCrae* by Linda Granfield

3. State your topic.

> Hope is a quiet thing. It is about believing in a dream, no matter how long and hard the road may be. Hope is a young man running across Canada to help find a cure for a disease that had caused so much hurting… Hope is the story of Terry Fox.
> —*Terry Fox* by Maxine Trottier

4. Use narration—a few lines of pertinent dialogue.

> It started with a Black-capped Chickadee. I was eight years old; the place was a country lane north of Toronto, where I grew up. On that cold November day, something caught my eye. It was a lively little ball of fluff, hopping from twig to twig in a leafless hedge. I forgot about the cold as I watched the agile little bird with the black cap and white cheeks.
> —*Backyard Birds* by Robert Bateman

5. Be different. Use startling words, expressions, or a little-known fact.

> Math lessons are full of problems…but English lessons are quite another story. Music lesson can break all records…but Geography lessons have their ups and downs. Chemistry lessons can be a gas…but Biology lessons are full of life. P.E. lessons are one long game…but History! History is horrible! Horrible dates to remember, horrible kings fighting horrible battles…
> —*Awesome Egyptians* by Terry Deary & Peter Hepplewhite

6. Restate your title and/or thesis sentence.

> Skating is the most important skill in hockey.
> —*Skating for Power & Speed* by Sean Rossiter & Paul Carson

7. State that you or somebody else once had an experience that the reader will find interesting or informative.

> In 1916, an American inventor named Louis Enricht announced that he had discovered a cheap additive that turned ordinary tap water into automotive fuel.
> —*Scams!* by Andreas Schroeder

Overview of Story Elements

Whether the lead uses a question, a powerful emotion, an unusual image, a clear statement, a quotation, or a first-person account to begin, once you hook your reader, the next step is to give details that connect to the main idea.

In *Chester's Masterpiece*, the egomaniacal cat wants to write his own story—he just needs to get pesky author-illustrator Mélanie Watt out of the way. But after several attempts Chester's writing goes astray. Children learn about the creative process and that a good story contains the following elements:

- setting
- action
- hero (or main character)
- characters (other than the hero: villains, sidekicks, etc.)
- an ending

Nailing Story Structure

All stories need a protagonist, and antagonist, and a conflict. I explain it this way to older kids,

> *Your protagonist is the main character, or your hero. Your protagonist must always want something. You also need an antagonist who gets in the protagonist's way. The plot is what happens between the protagonist and the antagonist. It involves conflict. The climax occurs when your protagonist is the last place in the world he/she wants to be.*

Teach kids how to create a beginning, middle, and end to a story. Use good books to show kids how authors develop character, setting, plot, conflict, and action. Analyze structural concepts together and have them practice writing constantly.

Writing Tip from Mem Fox
(author of *Possum Magic, Time for Bed, Reading Magic, Ten Little Fingers and Ten Little Toes*)

"DO NOT assume that plot is the most important element is a story, or even the only important element in a story. Character comes first. Next comes the precise choice of words and the correct rhythmic placement of those words. Then *trouble…*" (memfox.com)

Describing the Setting

Setting = Time + Place

All stories have a setting. In fiction, setting includes the time and location in which a story takes place. It initiates the main backdrop and mood for a story. Setting can play a key role in plot, as it does in man-vs-nature or man-vs-society stories. In some stories, the setting becomes a character itself.

Beginning writers often concentrate on people or events, but give little notice to where or when their stories take place. Kids can easily address the element of setting. Some students write stories that happen in their neighborhood, home, or school. Others use spectacular locations like the moon or Disneyworld. If you show students *how* experienced writers set the scene, they learn ways to establish settings in their stories.

In Grade 4, my son came home from school and announced, "I have to write a letter to Zach."

"Who's Zach?" I asked.

"He's this kid in a book we're reading."

"What book?"

"*Ticket to Curlew*," he said.

I am familiar with that title from working in the children's book industry. "Celia Barker Lottridge won a historical fiction award for that novel." I said. "It's about a boy and his dad settling into pioneer life on the prairie."

"I know. We read the story. Now I have to reread it, looking for words that describe the scene. Then I have to write a letter to his cousin Zach and tell him about it."

What a good idea! My son's teacher was helping her class get a feel for setting. In *Ticket to Curlew*, the year is 1915 and the place is Curlew, Alberta. When Sam Ferrier and his father arrive by train to build a new home, Sam sees endless stretches of grass and wonders why his father ever decided to bring the family to this barren land. Here's how Lottridge describes the setting from Sam's point of view:

> He saw one street with small wooden buildings straggling along it... The street was dirt with deep ruts that must have been made in mud time… there was not a single tree anywhere…

Indeed, Lottridge develops a strong sense of time and place. After studying how she does this, kids can practice describing their settings in more detail. Below, most of the words and phrases Cory used in his letter come from the author's depiction of setting:

April 15, 1915

Dear Cousin Zach,

I miss Jericho. A person in Curlew named Chalkey said that I'll have to walk five miles just to go to school!

Curlew must be the tiniest town in the world, it's so…so…silent and empty. There's only one street and the sidewalk is narrow compared to Jericho's.

The land around Curlew is dry and dusty, let me tell you! It has long, rippling grass, no landmarks (i.e., trees) and the horizon look to be miles away. All we see are stretches of flat land and blue sky.

It's lonely here on the prairie. There are no settlers or ploughed fields in this new land. Well, I miss not having any friends or family close by. Please write soon.

Your cousin,

Sam F.

"Setting a scene—providing proper lighting, the colors and textures of things, sounds—is one of my favorite things about writing a novel."
— Kevin Henkes

No matter where or when a story takes place, writers need to help readers feel like they are right there. If students know how authors do this, they grasp the concept more easily when writing their own stories.

Recently, I attended the Ontario Library Association Super Conference, and visited the publishers' exhibits. At one booth, I spotted the latest installment of The Boy Sherlock Holmes series and began reading. Another woman arrived.

"Is that the new Shane Peacock?" she asked, excitedly.

I raised my head and nodded.

"My kids love these books," she explained. "I work as a librarian. This writer is so good! He's won all kinds of awards."

I smiled. I know about Shane Peacock because older students often identify him as a favorite author. When they do, I want to find out why.

"What do you like about Shane Peacock's writing?" I once asked a Grade 6/7 class.

"He has the skill to conjure up foggy 1800s London on the page," one boy stated.

His stunning response captures how kids look up to good writers as role models. Kids sometimes amaze me with their answers. Obviously, Peacock's text awes and inspires this student. I marvel at the verbal recommendation he gives his peers. In order to make the most out of this opportunity, I read a passage aloud from *Eye of the Crow*:

> As the sun climbs, its rays spread light through the lifting yellow fog filtering down upon a brown, flowing mass of people: on top hats and bonnets, heavy clothes and boots swarming on bridges and along cobblestone streets. Hooves strike the pavement, clip-clopping over the rumbling iron wheels, the drone of the crowds, and hawkers' cries. The smell of horses, of refuse, of coal and gas, hangs in the air. Nearly everyone has somewhere to go on this late spring morning in the year of our Lord, 1867.

See how Shane Peacock sets the scene? His depiction evokes fog, squalor, and the London street smells. Showing instead of telling, writing with nouns and verbs, and filling the reader with sensory details—sights, sounds, tastes, smells and feelings—lead to this compelling writing.

When we give students a feel for setting, we help them grow as writers. Read books together with your class, highlighting words that give a strong sense of place and time. Create a chart in your room like the one below, so that students always have access to examples. As the year progresses, add setting descriptions from your reading. Then, when you ask students for more details about setting in their stories, they understand and can apply what they know.

EXAMPLES OF SETTING

Book	Author	Setting	Description
Ticket to Curlew	Celia Barker Lottridge	1915: prairies	• *one street with small wooden buildings straggling along it...The street was dirt with deep ruts that must have been made in mud time...there was not a single tree anywhere.* • *No signs of settlers: no houses, no trees, not even a ploughed field*
Firewing	Kenneth Oppel	Summer/ night/ forest	• *It had rained during the day* • *Now, under a three-quarter moon, the forest was silver with mist* • *Things always smell better after the rain* • *humid summer air*

This Can't Be Happening!	Gordon Korman	MacDonald Hall	• *East of Toronto, just off Highway 48, a beautiful, tree-lined campus across the road from famous Miss Scrimmage's Finishing School for Young Ladies.* • *Macdonald Hall…ivy-covered stone buildings and beautiful rolling lawns* • *most respected boarding school for boys…*
Holes	Louis Sachar	Camp Green Lake	• *There is no lake at Camp Green Lake. There once was a very large lake here, the largest lake in Texas. That was over a hundred years ago. Now it is just a dry, flat wasteland.*
Song and Dance Man	Karen Ackerman	Grandpa's attic	• *Steep, wooden steps* • *Faded posters of Grandpa hang on the walls.* • *Cardboard boxes, a rack of Grandma's winter dresses* • *Dusty brown, leather-trimmed trunk in the corner* • *The smell of cedar chips and old things*

For "setting" practice, one teacher asks his students

Describe a place where you felt so happy you want to go there again. Choose words that will help your readers feel as content as you did.

Blue and white houses, sandy beaches. Uh...this is the life. Imagine, lying on your striped beach towel, smooth sand in between your toes. The only sound is the waves crashing down on the beach. Almost sounds sureal doesn't it? But no, I experienced all this and more on my vacation to Cape Cod. When there, you can see cute seafood resturents, sea life and more. Next time you need a relaxing vacation think of 2 words, Cape Cod.

Sophie, a Grade 5 student, writes a newspaper called *The Awesome School Times*. She includes headlines, articles, editorials, letter to the editor, entertainment news, a sports column, classified ads, a comic strip, and more. A summer vacation in Cape Cod inspired her to write the piece on page 47.

Sophie conjures up an appealing image. We can hear the contentment in her voice. She uses descriptive words, her senses (sight, sound, and feel), and plenty of details to set the scene.

Writing Tip from Maxine Trottier

Many of award-winning author Maxine Trottier's books are set long ago, such as *Alone in an Untamed Land* (set in 1666). Others take place far away, like *Little Dog Moon*, which tells the story of a young monk living in 20th-century Nepal. Trottier suggests, "Try to visualize the setting in your mind's eye. Your readers have to use their imaginations, so feed those imaginations details about sights, sounds, smells and textures."

Bringing Characters to Life

Copy Real People

To create characters that seem real, encourage students to study people. Think about people they know. Then use their insights into these people to give characters life. Specific details include

A defect or flaw. For example, we believe the March sisters in *Little Women*, and like them more for their imperfections: literary Jo her temper and outspokenness, domesticated Meg her greed and envy of other people's wealth, musical Beth her overwhelming shyness, and artistic Amy her vanity and selfishness.

Emotions. For example, naughty Max in *Where the Wild Things Are*: sent to bed with no supper, Max feels so angry that his bedroom turns into a jungle, the walls dissolve, and he makes for a sailing boat on the ocean. Another example: Jim's terror when Ben Gunn first grabs him in *Treasure Island*.

Friends and relatives. For example, Matthew and Marilla Cuthbert: the elderly brother and sister live in Avonlea and adopt red-haired freckle-faced 11-year-old Anne Shirley. Other good examples from this book include Anne's best friend Diana Barry and her two nemeses: the hypercritical Mrs. Rachel Lynde and Gilbert Blythe, who calls her Carrots.

Goals. For example, Harry Potter: the 10-year-old's desire to live with his parents. Another example: Charlie Bucket's longing to buy a prize-winning Wonka Bar in *Charlie and the Chocolate Factory*.

Habits and quirks. For example, *Alice in Wonderland* has a hookah-smoking caterpillar, a duchess who gives her baby pepper and calls it a pig, a cat that disappears leaving only its smile, and a mad hatter.

Hobbies. For example, Mr. McGregor, the vegetable gardener in *The Tale of Peter Rabbit*.

Physical characteristics. For example, Jacob Two-Two is small and quiet, so he has to say everything twice to be heard over his brothers and sister. Other examples: Edward Lear's *Complete Nonsense Books* include an old man with a beard, the Pobble who has no toes, and the Dong with a luminous nose; Pippi Longstocking is famous for her red braids that stick out sideways.

Possessions. For example, a ring handed down through many generations.

Problems. Your main character (the protagonist) must want something. For example, Dorothy wants to get back to Kansas when a cyclone drops her and Toto in the land of Munchkins. On the way, she meets a scarecrow who wants a brain, a cowardly lion who wants courage, and a tin man who wants a heart.

Secrets. For example, in *The Secret Garden*, just who can hear Mary crying in the night?

Skills. For example, Dr. Dolittle can talk to animals; Mary Poppins can slide up banisters and float in the air; Rumpelstiltskin can spin straw into gold.

Values. For example, the much-tried loyalty of Ratty, Mole, and Badger toward the irrepressible Mr. Toad in *The Wind and the Willows*; the kindness of three old women in *A Wrinkle in Time*; a horse's bravery, goodness, and patience in *Black Beauty*.

Actions: Show your characters in action. Use action to dramatize personality traits. Instead of describing your character as angry, show the character acting angrily. For example, Kenneth Oppel depicts Captain Tritus, an irate man, like this:

> Captain Tritus was in a foul mood, his mouth clenching a cigarette on one side, and on the other muttering darkly about how was he expected to pay and feed his crew on an empty belly (*Skybreaker*: 1)

Use Dialogue

Popular children's author Gordon Korman says, "Dialogue reveals things about a character and moves a story along." He advises writers to spend time developing their characters, making them real by paying attention to the small details. Writers need to nail the dialogue in order for the characters to believable.

Many writers say eavesdropping helps to develop an ear for dialogue. Find a place to sit within earshot of other people and jot down bits of dialogue. Notice how people communicate.

- Do they explain a lot or make it brief?
- Do they talk in complete sentences or fragments?
- How does rhythm enter into everyday speech?

Also, pay attention to how little it takes to understand what they're talking about. Dialogue should operate in the same way: communicating a lot, but spelling out very little.

Writing Tip from Barbara Haworth-Attard
(author of *Forget-Me-Not, Theories of Relativity, Irish Chain, Flying Geese, Love-Lies-Bleeding*)

Eavesdrop! Author Barbara Haworth-Attard recommends it: "Listen to the conversations around you: in the playground yard, bus, classroom and at home. Most people have a rhythm in their speech or a favorite word they use all the time."

Use Names

What's in a name? Everything, if you want memorable characters. All fiction writers face this challenge. From Eoin Colfer's criminal mastermind Artemis Fowl to J.K. Rowling's Headmaster of Hogwarts Albus Dumbledore, most of the unforgettable characters in fiction have unusual names. I've always liked Miss Viola

Swamp, "the new teacher" in Harry Allard and James Marshall's *Miss Nelson is Missing!*

Think of the originality of character names from the first Harry Potter Book: Albus Dumbledore, Draco Malfoy, Hermione Granger, Lord Voldemort, Lucius Malfoy, Peeves, Professor Sprout, Ruebus Hagrid, Crookshanks, Hermes, Rita Skeeter, and Ron Weasley. As well as being imaginative, many of these names have "hidden meanings" to add extra interest.

Arthur Slade, author of the award-winning novel *Dust* says,

> If I give my characters a name then I can imagine them more easily. If my character's first name is Newton, then he might be scientific. Then I put them into a situation. Let's say Newton is haunted by a ghost. If he's the scientific type, will he believe in ghosts? My goal is to make my characters so real, that they walk out of the book and into the reader's mind.

Consider these suggestions to help students develop character names:

- Ethnicity. Choose a name consistent with your character's origins if it relates to the story.
- Personality. How strongly do you want the name to reflect the personality of your character?
- Genre. What kind of writing is it? (e.g., fantasy, action-adventure)
- Tone. What level of humor or seriousness does the writing have?

Some writers give names to their characters for personal reasons. The character resembles someone they know, or the name has a special meaning for them.

Occasionally authors use alliteration in naming their characters:

Bilbo Baggins, protagonist of *The Hobbit*
Junie B. Jones, feisty first grader
Jillian Jiggs, full of boundless energy and imagination
Beatrice Baudelaire, mother in Lemony Snicket's Series of Unfortunate Events
Dudley Dursley, first cousin of Harry Potter
Scaredy Squirrel, who never leaves his nut tree
Bruno and Boots, two friends with hilarious misadventures at Macdonald Hall
Maniac Magee, talented athlete and knot-untying specialist
Henry Huggins, who has fun adventures with his dog Ribsy
Doctor Dolittle, who shuns human patients in favor of animals
Billy Bones, pirate in *Treasure Island*
Willy Wonka, candy maker in *Charlie and the Chocolate Factory*

As well, many characters from comic books have alliteration in their names, including

Lois Lane, Superman's girlfriend
Peter Parker, Spider-Man
Green Goblin, Spider-Man's archenemy
Matthew Michael Murdock, Daredevil
Doctor Doom, Iron Man's nemesis
Susan Storm of the Fantastic Four

Occasionally students have difficulty naming characters in their writing. If so, invite them to a large or small group brainstorming session. Kids think of great ideas when they collaborate.

For a group activity, use a telephone directory to find unusual and interesting names. Encourage students to collect unusual names just for fun.

Organizing Ideas

Sometimes, writers lose focus and wander off into other topics. Graphic organizers such as webs, charts, sketches, storyboards, and lists help writers manage their thoughts. Later, students can see if they've stayed on topic by rereading their work. Does it make sense?

Observation Chart

You can create an observation chart for students to use when organizing sensory details. This sample is from the description of Cape Cod on page 47.

Topic: *Cape Cod*				
Sight	**Sound**	**Touch/Feel**	**Taste**	**Smell**
• *Blue and white houses* • *Sandy beaches* • *Striped beach towel* • *Cute seafood restaurants* • *Sea life*	• *Waves crashing down on the beach*	• *Smooth sand between your toes* • *Relaxing*		

Web

Webs help students think of subtopics to explore. This sample is from the Lego speech on page 25.

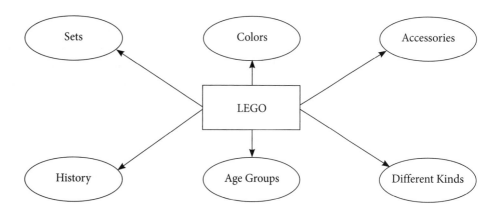

A web can act as a starting point for moving on to point-form notes.

History
- wooden at first
- passed down through the generations
- lego = Leg oht = play well
Sets
- Pirates, Knights, Kingdom, Space, Arctic, Police, Fire Station, Townspeople, Rescue
Colors
- red, blue, green, grey, orange, yellow, black, clear, white, brown, fluorescent, pink
Accessories
- magnets, cloth, string, firearms, medieval weapons, tools, money, wheels, men, women, armor, helmets, hats, wigs, mugs, glasses, computers, trolleys, eating utensils, shields, wands, capes, beards, umbrellas, animals

Plot Organizer

See page 57 for reproducible Plot Organizer.

This sample is from the story Rescue at Gold Point on page 97.

Plot Organizer

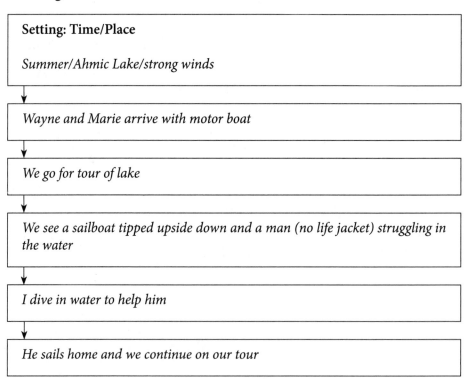

Setting: Time/Place

Summer/Ahmic Lake/strong winds

Wayne and Marie arrive with motor boat

We go for tour of lake

We see a sailboat tipped upside down and a man (no life jacket) struggling in the water

I dive in water to help him

He sails home and we continue on our tour

Headings

In nonfiction, headings help writers move through the text and keep it organized. They help readers navigate text quickly to find sections that interest them. Illustrations and captions also give a fuller idea about what to expect.

For headings that appeal to the ear, students can use wordplay: alliteration, rhyme, pun, or even a nod to their favorite author. As well, they can ask questions or use keywords in their headings.

Point out interesting headings as you read aloud nonfiction together. Encourage students to practice creating good headings in their fact-based writing.

Bullet Points

For more on bullets, see page 111 in Chapter 7: Visual Presentation.

Gone are the days of long sentences in long paragraphs. Readers want information fast. Teach older students how to present information in bulleted lists. Students can use bullet points to list features, steps, or tips. Bullet points make you a stronger writer, if you're good at writing them. In fact, being good at writing bullets is an important writing skill. Bullets help draw people back to parts they skimmed, give support details, and present information powerfully.

Whenever possible, I spend time with my nieces. As they grow, I enjoy seeing what books they like and hearing about interesting school activities. This past visit, our conversation led to how they've used bullet points in their classes.

Laura said, "In Grade 5, our teacher taught us to use bullet points in expository writing. We used them for topics that have no chronological order. The class brainstormed subjects each person could relate to, such as Safety Rules in the Kitchen, Favorite Summer Activities, or Things to Keep in Mind While Walking a Dog. We focused broad subjects into simpler groups, such as Water Activities or Fun Foods in the Summer. Once we had topics, we would list four or five bullet points using descriptive words and well-formed phrases." For example, here is one of Laura's lists:

Thing to Keep in Mind While Walking a Dog

- be familiar with the area
- bring a bag
- know leash laws
- watch dog for signs of exhaustion
- pick up after dog

Sophie's Grade 6 class used bullets points in their explanatory writing. First, they read a piece on earthworms. Then they picked out key points and used bullets to extract important information. The teacher taught them to write just key words, not the whole sentence. They used the bullets to group topics for further elaboration:

Earthworms

- Dietary Needs
- Habitat
- How They Help Us

Then they wrote paragraphs in their own words.

Laura added, "In Grade 8 we compiled information in chart or table form. We'd use bullet points to organize our thoughts. For example, we made a chart of mythological figures. The bullet points became a study tool."

When you're doing jot notes, instead of writing word-for-word sentences, use bullet points for quickly organizing ideas. Students can use bullet points for

- brainstorming
- studying
- organizing
- grouping
- listing

Block Buster

Bullet points make life easier for writers. They help organize your thoughts and provide efficiency. With bullet points, simple structures work well. You can list key things without worrying about how your sentences flow from one item to the next.

How to Conclude

Have you ever read a book that you wished would not end? If you enjoy reading something, you take your time finishing it. You know it's almost over, but you're sad for it to finish—and you hope it ends in a satisfying way. Ask your students to name books that they didn't want to end. What did they like about these books? What did they think about the endings?

Good endings do two things:

1. wrap up the story
2. give the reader something to think about and leave a lasting memory.

Explain to kids that endings should make a final impression upon the reader. In fiction, sometimes authors end their stories with a memory, a feeling, a wish, or a hope. Other times they end the story by referring back to the beginning. Students can study the characteristics of good endings in picture books. Then they can practice writing good endings for their own narratives.

"Paradise lost is sometimes heaven found" is the closing line in *Hey, Al*, a wonderful book by Arthur Yorinks. Al is a janitor who is unhappy with his life. One day a bird appears at the window promising to take him to a better place. Of course, something that sounds that good probably isn't.

For other picture books with good endings, try Chris Van Allsburg. He is a master at surprise endings, circular endings, and "write the next chapter in your head" endings. I also suggest *When the Relatives Come* by Cynthia Rylant for its circular opening and closing.

In nonfiction, the concluding paragraph reviews what the writer has covered along with a final comment about the main point.

The conclusion (ending or closing) wraps things up for the reader. Teach kids to stop writing when they have said everything, and tie up all loose ends. Following are ideas on how to write a good conclusion.

"There must be something to think about at the end."
— Chris Van Allsburg

More picture books with good endings:
Stellaluna by Janell Cannon
Something From Nothing by Phoebe Gilman
The Tin Heart by Karen Ackerman
Fly Away Home by Eve Bunting
The Stranger by Chris Van Allsburg

Five Ways to End a Story

Tips for Ending
- Stop writing when you have said everything.
- Tie up the loose ends.
- Be sure to have at least three sentences in your conclusion, whatever type it may be.

1. Question

Close with a question. You can answer it, or leave it for the reader to decide.
Example: *It was the worst experience of his life. Andrew decided that he would never go on a roller coaster again. Who can blame him?*

2. Quotation

Close by quoting a character in the story or someone you know personally.
Example: *"You're going to regret this." Those were Sheila's last words as I pulled her into the rollercoaster seat. I now know she was serious.*

3. Personal Comment

Close with a comment or response to what you have written. This is different from giving an opinion. It is a personal conclusion you have reached or a lesson you have learned because of the experience you wrote about.
Example: *Never will I ride a rollercoaster with someone who is a "chicken" again. I should have listened when Sheila said she was afraid of them. Next time I will know better.*

4. Beginning of a New Story

You can close with a hint of things to come, or the beginning of a new story—a sequel of sorts.
Example: *He was exhausted. It had been a long and difficult week. Robert closed his eyes and thought of the many other adventures that lie ahead.*

5. Mystery

Close with a statement that shows some things will never be resolved.
Example: *We watched Bill walk down the road until he became just a tiny speck and then disappeared altogether into the twilight. He was gone. That was the last time any of us ever saw him.*

Seven Ways to End Nonfiction Writing

1. Question

The question must relate to the main idea.
Example: *Are we going to let this situation continue?*

2. Quotation

Close with a quotation from a famous person. Relate it to your topic, and use the Internet or books for sources.
Example: *"Never use two words when one will do."—Thomas Jefferson*

3. Generalize

Take a broad view without making a choice of one thing over another.
Example: *Hard to say, but at least this much seems clear: a scam, if it's entertaining enough can be enjoyed by its victims – and readers!* (from *Scams!* by Andreas Schroeder)

4. Summarize

Close with a summary of your main ideas.
Example: *As you can see, it helps to know how to find the answer. Never rely on a teacher to be nearby. Learn how to research so you can find a solution.*

5. Strong Statement

Make a choice. Close with a statement that forcefully states your opinion.
Example: *Deal with criminals, no matter his/her age, according to the crime. The legal system is too lenient on juvenile offenders. Criminals should not be free because they are juveniles.*

6. Open Conclusion

State that you have presented the facts, and let the reader make up his or her mind.
Example: *Some statistics show that young drivers are more dangerous than older drivers. Other statistics show the opposite. Therefore, which drivers are the most dangerous is still debatable.*

7. Suggestions for Further Learning

List other web sites, essays, articles, or books for the reader to further his/her knowledge of the subject.

A Concluding Thought on Organization

Like any skill, organizing a piece of writing improves with time and practice. Students need time to think, write, and rewrite. Thinking and writing go together. Kids need time to learn about the subject, and organize the information. After you teach how to write strong leads, place information in order and write a strong conclusion, they will be able to better organize their writing.

"Work extra hard on the beginning of your story, so it snares readers instantly. And know how you're going to end your story before you start writing; without a sense of direction, you can get lost in the middle."
—Joan Lowery Nixon (author of *The Kidnapping of Christina Lattimore, The Other Side of Dark*)

Plot Organizer

Setting: Time/Place

Pembroke Publishers © 2010 *How Bullets Saved My Life* by Judy Green ISBN 978-1-55138-255-5

3

Voice

> *The golden rule of writing is to write what you care about. If you care about your topic, you'll do your best writing, and then you stand the best chance of really touching a reader in some way.*
> —Jerry Spinelli ("Quotes")

Voice is the heart and soul of writing—the writer's thoughts and feelings coming out in the words. Strong voice gives writing personality and style. Through voice, a writer shows confidence, individuality, and perspective. Teachers can use this list to help young writers develop voice:

- Write honestly and from the heart
- Share your feelings about the topic
- Care about what you have written
- Give the reader a sense of who you are
- Connect with the reader

Why Is Voice Important?

Once I led a writing workshop for intermediate teachers and school principals. We began by discussing excellent children's authors—writers of picture books, nonfiction, fiction—and establishing what makes good writing. As I listed the characteristics of good writing, I said, "We look for interesting ideas, clear organization, appealing word choice, sentence fluency, conventions, and of course, 'strong voice.'"

One of the attending principals asked, "What do you mean by a *you-ish* voice?"

"Sound like yourself, rather than an encyclopedia," I answered.

Voice is how you "talk" in writing. Writing Traits expert Ruth Culham explains it as "the way a writer brings the topic to life, depending on the intended audience." Strong voice is engaging to read. Energy and emotions charge the writing so that it is compelling and full of conviction. The writer's tone is interesting and presence is powerful. Readers can "hear" personality in the writing.

A weak voice, on the other hand, creates a watered-down effect, where the writer seems indifferent to the subject or distanced from the audience. The writing is plain, and the author sounds monotonous, flat, or even bored. With a weak voice, a writer loses the reader's emotional investment.

Mem Fox and Lyn Wilkinson wrote a book called *English Essentials: the wouldn't-be-without-it guide to writing well.* They offer this insight about the elements of good writing:

The presence of voice will indicate to readers that above and beyond the sweat and the bother, the writer has actually enjoyed writing the piece. Voice reveals a lively commitment to the writing task, a desire to be read, a high level of care. Let your voice be heard. It will make your writing come alive.

Voice is difficult to pin down in writing. Just understanding it can be a challenge. Before we get into how to teach it to students, let's compare strong voice to weak voice in chart form.

STRONG VOICE VS WEAK VOICE

Strong Voice	Weak Voice
Writing is compelling, authentic, and engaging; tone is interesting; you hear the writer's conviction	Writing is plain; writer is indifferent, distanced from topic and/or audience
Writer connects with audience. Writer's devotion comes through in the text	Writer sounds flat, bored, unaware of audience; reader loses interest
Expository writing is committed, persuasive	Expository writing lacks commitment
Narrative writing is honest, engaging, personal	Narrative writing shows no attempt at voice

Understandably, the concept of voice intimidates young writers. Some students require help adding voice to their writing. Like the principal in my workshop, they need a clear understanding of what strong voice sounds like. Once they know what voice means, it becomes easier to grasp.

Recently I read aloud *Chester's Masterpiece* to the uproarious laughter of primary children. When Mélanie Watt's cat Chester attempts to write his own masterpiece, a duel ensues. This is a good book for teaching voice. Words like "artistic expression" and "mime" challenge primary kids, but they can easily distinguish between exasperated Mélanie —"Chester, what are you up too???" "Chester, this is unacceptable!" "Chester!!! That's not funny!"—and bossy Chester—"This is MY BOOK! I can write whatever I want! AND I can draw all over the pages and make up MY own stories!" Obviously, these two characters sound different. They use different kinds of language: different words, tone, sentences, and forms of address.

You can use the Chester books by Mélanie Watt to teach the following lessons:
- voice
- story elements (page 44)
- titles (page 83)
- visual presentation (page 109)
- protagonist, antagonist, and conflict (page 44)

Voice is the individual style you use that gives your writing personality. Your voice establishes the tone and sets it apart from other writing. This applies as much in writing nonfiction as it does in fiction.

I'm writing this book in a friendly, conversational voice. I want to sound the way I would speak if we were chatting face-to-face. Encourage students to think of writing as chatting with someone. Use your talking voice but, instead of speaking aloud, write words. Sounding like yourself has a conversational effect. As you write, let your author's voice shine. How do your words sound? Look at

- tone: Is it friendly, formal, chatty, or distant?
- word choice: Do you use everyday words or high-brow language?
- sentence patterns: Are they varied, or do they repeat?
- personality: What do you show about yourself?

Teachers can demonstrate voice by reading aloud. Some picture books, like *The True Story of the Three Little Pigs* by Jon Scieszka, appeal to all grade levels and make good teaching tools for voice. In this hilarious twist on the original story, kids can identify the wolf's sarcastic and impassioned voice. After hearing several examples of strong voice, kids can practice it in their own writing.

Doctor De Soto is another excellent read-aloud to teach voice. As is usual for William Steig—who also wrote *Shrek, Sylvester and the Magic Pebble* and *Abel's Island*—his tone is matter-of-fact. Sounding like himself was important to William Steig.

The following piece describes Martha Parravano's experience reading *Doctor De Soto* to her daughters:

> I found myself experimenting with different inflections and different voices each time I read the book (once even reading Doctor De Soto's invitation to the fox to try his "remarkable preparation" in the sing-songy come-on voice of a carnival huckster). The all-too-human fox, with his wimpy aversion to pain ("'Please!' the fox wailed. 'Have mercy, I'm suffering!'"") and ridiculously short gratefulness-span ("On his way home, he wondered if it would be shabby of him to eat the De Sotos when the job was done") provided much comic relief and opportunity for exaggerated villainous voices. (Parravano, 2010)

Popular Picture Books with Strong Voice

Picture books can help demonstrate different ways that authors express their voice. The following titles represent a variety of voices—from bossy and self-absorbed to kind and gentle. Teachers can use these books at all grade levels to show the power of voice.

Amazing Grace by Mary Hoffman: Grace wants to be Peter Pan in the school play and learns that you can be anything you want.

A Bad Case of Stripes by David Shannon: A little girl feels so concerned with everyone's opinion that she stops being herself.

Chester by Mélanie Watt: Mélanie tries to write a story about a mouse, but her cat keeps interfering.

Chrysanthemum by Kevin Henkes: Chrysanthemum loves her name until everyone giggles about it at school.

Doctor De Soto by William Steig: Can the well-respected mouse-dentist outsmart a wily fox?

Lilly's Purple Plastic Purse by Kevin Henkes: Lilly loves school until her teacher disciplines her in class.

The Memory String by Eve Bunting: Laura struggles to accept her dad's new girlfriend years after the death of her mom.

The True Story of the Three Little Pigs by Jon Scieszka: A twist on the original story of *The Three Little Pigs*—as told by the wolf.

You're Mean, Lily Jean by Frieda Wishinsky: Carly always played with her big sister. Then Lily Jean moved in next door.

Where the Wild Things Are by Maurice Sendak: An angry boy's feelings and fantasies upon being sent to bed without any supper.

I've listed a few picture books with strong voice; you will find endless possibilities. When other titles reveal the author's true self, add them to your list.

The Elusive Adolescent Voice

How do we help older kids let their voice shine? Teaching voice can be especially challenging with older students. I've learned that as they get older, some kids try to hide their feelings. In my workshops the Grade 7–8 students typically act less lively, are less forthcoming than the younger kids. Their remoteness is a conditioned response. One teacher explained that adolescents feel afraid to say they like something for fear of their peers' reactions. They clam up and harden their shell. Knowing that writers feel vulnerable at the best of times, and that adolescents are especially self-conscious, we must encourage them to sound natural in their writing.

To show the importance of voice in nonfiction, I like to read from the *Horrible Histories* series by Terry Deary, humorous informational books on the Middle Ages, Greeks, Romans, Vikings, and Egyptians. Whereas some history books are dull, dry, and wordy, these books engage readers. As I read aloud, I invite kids to describe the writer's voice. "He's entertaining, funny, excited, and enthusiastic," they say. "Everything the writer says, he means." That's the conviction we refer to when we talk about strong voice.

The *Horrible Histories* series features other strategies for writing interesting nonfiction:

- the headings use alliteration that enlivens dull text: "Gruesome Grave Robbers," "A Gallery of Gods," "Phascinating Pharaohs" (see page 84)
- the information is accurate, yet quirky (see Chapter 2: Organization)
- the words are clear and concise (see Chapter 4: Word Choice)
- puns, word play, jokes, and funny details add to the appeal (see Chapter 4: Word Choice)

Show students these strategies, so they can practice them in their nonfiction writing.

Master storyteller Christopher Paul Curtis captures our attention with voice in his YA novel, *Elijah of Buxton*. Eleven-year-old Elijah is the first child born into freedom in Buxton, Canada, a settlement of runaway slaves just over the border from Detroit. In this conversation, Eli meets his friend Cooter, who explains that he has a mystery:

"I was cutting through M'deah's truck path and seen some tracks that I ain't never seen afore."
"What kind of tracks? Were they big?"
"Uh-uh, they's long and wiggly. I followed 'em but they disappeared in the grass."

After his mother chastises him for screaming that hoop snakes have invaded Buxton, gullible Elijah says, "But, Ma, I ain't looking to die even one time, 'specially not from no hoop snake bite! It's better to get your head blowed off!"

Then he confesses to readers "…being fra-gile's the biggest bone Ma's got to pick with me. There ain't nothing in the world she wants more than for me to quit being so doggone fra-gile."

See how Curtis grabs the reader? His presence is powerful: you hear his heart and soul in the story. His writing has realness, a human quality—an authenticity—about it. Elijah admits his fragility. The writing is personal, honest, and engaging. "His voice adds so much to the story," one girl said. "He writes in a way that you can see it happening. It could be true."

Equally, Polly Horvath lures us in with a lively voice in *Everything on a Waffle*:

> My name is Primrose Squarp. I am eleven years old. I have hair the color of carrots in an apricot glaze (recipe to follow), skin fair and clear where it isn't freckled, and eyes like summer storms.

Use *Everything on a Waffle* to teach adolescents about voice. The text has energy and wit. Primrose is obviously likeable, insightful, vulnerable, and comical. The tone is interesting and appropriate for the audience. As well, kids can identify interesting descriptions such as "hair the color of carrots in an apricot glaze" and the simile "eyes like summer storms."

As always, teach a variety of writing strategies with one book. Picture books, diaries, and novels written in the first person—such as *Elijah of Buxton* and *Everything on a Waffle*—make good resources for showing older kids strong voice.

How to Teach Voice

Generate a list of emotions. These words reveal different voices in literature. As you read stories together during the year, discuss what mood or personality you sense in the "voices."

Anger	Exhaustion	Pride
Amusement	Fear	Regret
Annoyance	Frustration	Relief
Anticipation	Gratitude	Remorse
Anxiety	Greed	Reluctance
Arrogance	Guilt	Resentful
Boredom	Happiness	Sadness
Compassion	Hatred	Satisfaction
Concern	Haughty	Scared
Confidence	Hopeful	Shame
Confusion	Humble	Shock
Contentment	Hunger	Shy
Cowardly	Impatience	Sly
Curiosity	Indifference	Sorrow
Desperation	Indignation	Stubborn
Disappointment	Jealousy	Sullen
Disapproval	Joy	Surprise
Disgust	Loneliness	Sympathy
Embarrassment	Love	Unease
Empathy	Meek	Wary
Energetic	Overwhelmed	Worry
Enthusiasm	Panic	Wounded
Envy	Powerless	
Excitement	Defeated	

As you read various genres during the year, encourage your kids to identify what voice the author uses. Create a wall chart to reinforce the concept of voice, like this one:

VOICE

Book	Author	Genre	Voice
Doctor De Soto	William Steig	Picture book	Matter-of-fact
Awesome Egyptians (Horrible Histories)	Terry Deary	Nonfiction	Entertaining, funny, enthusiastic, excited
Elijah of Buxton	Christopher Paul Curtis	Historical Fiction	Real, human-like, vibrant
Everything on a Waffle	Polly Horvath	Fiction	Energetic, insightful, comical, vulnerable

Writing in a You-ish Voice

Students can complete the following statements with as much voice as possible.

- It makes me SAD when…
- The FUNNIEST thing that ever happened to me was…
- I get really ANGRY when…
- The most EXCITING thing I ever did was…
- The SCARIEST thing I remember is…

Then they can share what they have written. Put the strongest examples on a bulletin board as examples for writing that has voice.

When it comes to writing with voice, kids need to remember this:

- Voice is easier than it seems. Just be yourself.
- Think of your audience. Your voice changes as your audience changes. For example, the way you talk to your friends is different from how you speak to your parents. If you have no connection to the reader, pretend that you are writing for your best friend.
- Think of your topic. How do you feel about it? Put those feelings into your writing. Show your reader how you feel. Do not hold back!

Laura (Grade 6) embraces winter. In the following poem you can hear her rich voice, see why she loves this season, and feel her enjoyment. Strong verbs such as *tobogganing*, *sipping*, and *cuddling* add energy to her message. She even uses alliteration (*fun with my friends*, *snowy slopes*) to boost the sound.

Definition Poem

Winter is…
Tobogganing down snowy slopes,
Sipping marshmallowey hot chocolate,
Cuddling my dog by the fire,
Having fun with my friends
And just being outside in the fresh winter air!

Reflecting Experience

Voice reflects how your character experiences the world. Kids can practice by telling their stories or poems aloud. That way, they can let their characters tell the story. If kids can "hear" their characters, they'll get the voice right.

Laura also wrote an *I Am…* poem about a snowman. Her voice gives life to this writing:

<u>I Am Poem</u>

I am white and cold
I wonder why there's sun
I hear toboggans whooshing by
I see a winter wonderland
I want to be forever
I am white and cold

I pretend that I'm a kid
I feel shutout sometimes
I touch the cold snow
I worry about spring
I cry to think of melting
I am white and cold

I understand that I'll melt
I say "Winter Forever!"
I dream to see a summer
I try to hang on until fall
I hope this will be the year to stay
I am white and cold

At the beginning of this poem, we can hear the longing in Laura's voice. Her verbs—*wonder, want, pretend, worry, cry*—convey the snowman's feelings of despair. She contrasts these with feelings of optimism by using powerful verbs such as *understand, dream, try, hope*, in the third verse. Sensory details—what she hears, sees, and feels—add interest.

Developing Voice

Provide enjoyable opportunities to write as much as possible. Students can keep a journal. They can imagine writing letters to a friend. They can write about their day, the things they see and experience, the thoughts that go through their heads. They can write their views on current events. This is good voice practice, because it helps kids think of new things to say and ways to say them.

Once your kids have a collection of personal writing, get them to ask people how they sound on the page.

- Is my writing serious? funny? factual? upbeat? depressing? straightforward?
- Do I write my mind? Express opinions? Or do I use polite, politically correct words?
- Do I sound like *myself*?

We need to dig deep to uncover our real voices. That means knowing ourselves and what we think about the world.

Using Journal Writing

Diary writing comes from a long literary tradition—from *Anne Frank* to *Junie B. Jones*. The diary format remains popular at all levels of children's books. Typically, diary books have a young narrator writing in first person, with a conversational, rather than literary, style. Use them to help students get a feel for voice. Choose any diary or journal-type book to read to your students. Tune in to how the writer captures our attention through his/her personal style.

Primary kids love Junie B. Jones, the main character in Barbara Park's popular chapter books. This series helps build on the link between spoken and written language. Barbara Park writes in the voice of a feisty five-year-old. Junie B. is sassy, funny, and insightful. First-graders relate to her trials and tribulations. Says Barbara Park, "Kids like Junie B. because (like them) she isn't perfect. She makes mistakes, gets in trouble, and has a temper. All of these things make her seem more real."

Humor is a popular theme in the middle years. Boys and girls like the *Diary of a Wimpy Kid* books by Jeff Kinney. Greg Heffley fills his diary—or, as he emphasizes, "JOURNAL"—with funny illustrations and written descriptions of his day-to-day struggles with family and friends. What makes the series so popular? Kids relate to Greg, who deals with a variety of problems, many of his own making.

Dear Dumb Diary by Jim Benton is another funny and popular series for this age group. A middle-school girl named Jamie Kelly writes her diary in the first person. She encourages kids to make their own journals and write entries online. Here is an online excerpt:

> I know that your uncle's kids are your cousins, but then there are things like second cousins once-removed. What does that mean? "Cousins once-removed." I had a wart once removed. ("Make a Diary")

In Anne Mazer's series, *The Amazing Days of Abby Hayes,* 11-year-old Abby uses her diary to resolve frustrations, make quirky observations, and amuse herself. Kids like the author's unique style—how she writes with purple pen. When she does that, it means that she is writing in her journal. Kids say that when Abby writes in her journal, it is easier to relate to the character.

Novels in diary form remain a well-liked genre of young adult fiction. They typically feature a self-absorbed teenage narrator dealing with growing up. Some of the novels are frequently hilarious, such as *Alice, I Think* by Susan Juby. Others, like *Monster* by Walter Dean Myers, deal with painful issues and don't attempt to lighten their stories with humor.

Keep in mind that you can use books repeatedly to teach a variety of writing strategies. Diary or journal entries often feature:

- first person narration; i.e., "I" in the writing (see page 42)
- linking words to do with time. These examples come from the first few pages of *Diary of a Wimpy Kid*: *Today is…*, *Next period…*, *Nowadays…*, *Then one day…*, *A couple of days into summer vacation…*, *After Rodrick woke me up…*, *Yesterday…*
- action verbs. Strong verbs improve descriptive writing (see page 80). These examples come from *Alice, I Think*: *ditched, stopped, announced, veering, painted, impressed, pretending*

Books in Diary Format for Ages 4–8

Diary of a Worm by Doreen Cronin and Harry Bliss
Junie B. Jones series by Barbara Park

Books in Diary Format for Ages 8–12

Amelia series by Marissa Moss
The Diary of a Wimpy Kid series by Jeff Kinney
Dear Dumb Diary series by Jim Benton
Amazing Days of Abby Hayes series by Anne Mazer
Diary of a Would-Be Princess by Jessica Green
My Name is America series
My America series
Dear America series/*Dear Canada* series
Royal Diaries series

Books in Diary Format for Ages 12–16

Mable Riley by Marthe Jocelyn
Alice, I Think by Susan Juby
Monster by Walter Dean Myers
Youth in Revolt: The Journals of Nick Twisp

Books like these encourage children to keep a journal and help them make it a habit. Generally kids like being able to write about their life and add drawings—unless they resemble Greg Heffley. In *Diary of a Wimpy Kid*, Greg starts his journal by getting something straight:

> …this was MOM's idea, not mine. But if she thinks I'm going to write down my "feelings" in here of whatever, she's crazy. So just don't expect me to be all "Dear Diary" this and "Dear Diary" that."

Diaries offer students a platform to recount personal details. They also provide the opportunity to develop fluency—to keep ideas flowing (see Chapter 5: Fluency). We write diaries

- to retell events and experiences
- to record ideas, thoughts, and feelings

In journal writing, kids get ideas from their own lives. Because they are retelling events and experiences from daily life, they already know many details. This helps to develop their creativity, individuality, and voice. Clarify that you will be making personal rather than corrective comments on their thoughts and ideas. Try offering personal comments like these:

Excellent detail and expression of emotions!
Great communication and use of language

At the beginning of Grade 4, teacher Lynne Shuttleworth gave her students Reading Journals. In these lined notebooks, they wrote character sketches about fellow classmates and then storybook characters; summarized book chapters; took notes about figurative language; filled in genre reading charts; and kept a monthly reading log.

One month, she asked her students to read a poetry book, a nonfiction science book on light, a fantasy novel, and one free choice. In his journal, my son Cory made a chart of his reading. Under the *Title* heading, he wrote *Granny Squares*. Under the *Author* heading, he wrote "Mae Mist." Under the *Genre* heading he wrote "Poetry." He added a special note at the bottom of his chart: "Mae Mist is my great-grandmother."

Mrs. Shuttleworth wrote a personal comment back: "I'd like to read the book. What a great thing for you to have chosen."

Cory wrote, "Thanks."

Use diary writing as a versatile tool at school and home:

- To encourage kids to write without self-censorship or fear of failure
- To support good daily writing habits—the more you write, the better you get
- To develop voice

Dear Diary

When Junie B. Jones writes in her journal, she expresses her thoughts and feelings about the endless challenges of life as a first-grader. After you have read aloud a Junie B. book with your class, choose one to reread. This time, look closely at *how* Barbara Park wrote it. Read an excerpt from *Aloha-ha-ha!*, where Junie B. goes on vacation to Hawaii with her family:

Friday
Dear first-grade journal,
I'VE GOT BIG NEWS!
I'VE GOT BIG NEWS!
Last night Daddy told me a happy surprise. And it's calld my fiamily is going on an exciting vakashum vacation! And it is going to be the time of our life, I tell you!
I am trying to save my news for Show and Tell. But I don't think I can wait that long. That is how come I am going to ask my teacher to start that activity RIGHT EXACTLY NOW!
Please stand by…

See how Junie B. Jones uses her voice when she writes? Her energy and personality shine. Written in the first person, Junie B. provides a strong model for primary kids. Use it to introduce the idea of voice in writing:

- Notice that Junie B. uses true-to-life "kidspeak," and sometimes incorrect grammar, which adds to the humor.
- Note that she experiments with new words like "vacation."
- Point out that Junie B. narrates her stories; i.e., she uses words and phrases involving "I" (first-person). This allows us to see her point of view, including opinions, thoughts and feelings.
- Note that the story ideas come from everyday life. They recount daily experiences such as owning a pet, having to get glasses, dealing with tattletales, knowing monsters hide under the bed, getting in trouble for spying on someone, putting on a school play, and more.

The attention that comes from rereading and talking about these bulleted points will help children in their own writing.

Writing Tip from Carol Matas
(author of *Daniel's Story, Lisa, After the War*)

"When I was young I used my diary to write about the boys I liked. I also began to write poetry and confide my thoughts about life, relationships and whatever I wanted. It's a place where you can be honest and express yourself with no fear."

Read a diary or journal-type book to your students. Discuss the kinds of feelings, impressions, and observations the character shares in each entry. Then invite students to write journals about their daily life. They must do more than just tell what happened. Ask them to share feelings, impressions, and observations about events. Encourage them to be creative by including photos, poems, drawings, and song lyrics if they wish. Sometimes, they may like the results and want to turn their entries into complete stories.

Any journal format works, as long as it's appealing and easy to use. Kids can use notebooks or make and decorate their own journals.

Allow 5 to 15 minutes every day for your students to write entries. Periodically, ask volunteers to read aloud from their journals. Collect and read journals once a week, making personal comments on their thoughts and ideas.

Writing Tips from Barbara Park

"Sorry… but I'm afraid it's the same old advice everyone gives:
1) READ, READ, READ. You absorb so much about writing by reading a variety of authors.
2) PRACTICE, PRACTICE, PRACTICE. Keep journals…write poems and short stories… whatever.
But most of all….
3) WRITE ABOUT WHAT YOU LOVE. I love writing humor…but others prefer mysteries or fantasies. Writing should never be a drudge. So have fun with it!"

These four ideas help get kids to write in their diaries:

1. Practice with a friend or family member. Two writers can swap journals back and forth, writing responses to each other.
2. List favorite—or least favorite—things: books, authors, poems, rhymes, songs, foods, sports, people, and more. For example:

   My Favorite Authors
   1. Mélanie Watt (*Chester*)
   2. Kenneth Oppel (*Sunwing*, *Silverwing*, *Firewing* and *Darkwing*)
   3. Jerry Spinelli (*Loser*)
   4. J.K. Rowling (Harry Potter series)
   5. Gordon Korman (Macdonald Hall series)
   6. Shane Peacock (The Boy Holmes series)
   7. Christopher Paul Curtis (*Elijah of Buxton* and *Bud, Not Buddy*)
   8. William Steig (*Shrek* and *Doctor De Soto*)
   9. Louis Sachar (*Holes*)
   10. Jane Yolen (*Owl Moon*)
   11. Karen Ackerman (*Song and Dance Man*)
   12. James Marshall (*Miss Nelson is Missing*)
   13. Bill Martin Jr. (*Barn Dance!*)

3. List favorite—or least favorite—things about a particular month or season. For example:

   My Ten Favorite Things about January
   1. Drinking hot chocolate
   2. Reading good books on snowy nights
   3. Snow falling on cedars (Also the name of a prize-winning adult novel)
   4. Walking on frozen lakes
   5. Skiing
   6. Building snow forts
   7. Spotting cardinals
   8. Wearing warm sweaters
   9. Baking cookies
   10. Sitting by the fire

4. Focus on events, experiences, feelings, impressions, and observations. Make it a collage journal! In addition to practicing writing skills, paste pictures, ticket stubs and more onto the pages. See Journal-Writing Prompts on page 71.

I tell kids, "When you move from your journal into a story, think of it as a long letter to your reader. We rarely have problems writing letters and journals."

A Comment on Voice

"As a writer, you're obligated to draw readers into your world, and if your writing isn't interesting to them, you won't succeed."

— Donald Perry (author of *Life Above the Jungle Floor*)

Give kids lots of time and writing practice to develop voice. Impatient writers love to skip that part of the process. The tips in this chapter will set young writers on the right path to uncovering their voice—and, through that, find authentic voices for their characters and stories.

Journal-Writing Prompts

If you need ideas for your journal entries, try these:

Events and Plans

- This weekend, I…

- Today I…

- At recess, I…

- Last summer, I…

- Next winter, I…

Feelings and Favorites

- I get frustrated when…

- I dislike…

- My most embarrassing moment was…

- The best hiding place in my house is…

- My favorite author is…

If I Could…

- travel in a time machine, I would go to…

- be invisible for a day, I would…

- choose my bedtime, it would be…

- be good at any one thing, it would be…

- meet my favorite author, it would be…

Pembroke Publishers © 2010 *How Bullets Saved My Life* by Judy Green ISBN 978-1-55138-255-5

4

Word Choice

> *You need to readandreadandreadandread to learn as many different ways of using language as possible. You also need to read in order to build inside your head a massive bank of lusciously different words that you can choose from at any time.*
> —Mem Fox (memfox.com)

Word choice involves using rich, colorful, precise language to move and enlighten the reader. Specific words we choose create images, capture a reader's attention, and make our writing memorable. Teachers can suggest several strategies toward well-crafted writing:

- Find words that are "just right."
- Stretch to use new, interesting words.
- Think verbs, verbs, verbs (use high-energy words).
- Eliminate tired, trite words.
- Cut the fat: use only words that carry their own weight.

See Get the Words Right on page 88.

In Chapter 3, we saw how *Doctor De Soto* by William Steig exemplifies strong voice in literature. Steig is also famous for slipping in wonderful "big" words—such as *assistant*, *convulsions*, and *hoisted*—that children love to hear and that increase their vocabularies.

William Steig is revered as the creator of *Shrek!*, as well as dozens of other magnificent books. The humor lies in Steig's use of language. In *Shrek!*, an ugly ogre revels in his disgusting characteristics, and falls in love with the ugliest, smelliest, most horrific princess he's ever seen. They quote monster poetry to each other:

> Says the ogre, "Your horny warts, your rosy wens, like slimy bogs and fusty fens, thrill me."
>
> Says the princess, "Your lumpy nose, your pointy head, your wicked eyes, so livid red, just kill me."

This is great, great stuff. See how Steig challenges us with high-level vocabulary? He knows how to use the right word, in the right way, at the right time. His striking phrases are memorable. Good writers use specific words to create an intended effect, impression, or mood.

Teach students that word choice matters in the writing process. Begin by reading aloud picture books with powerful language. Explain to students that their choice of words provides a clue to their feelings; words can also provoke a feeling in the reader.

Michelle (Grade 5) uses rich, colorful, precise language to create stirring images in this couplet poem:

I raise my head toward the sky,
And watch an eagle soar on by.
Oh how I yearn to be up there,
And feel the wind rustle through my hair.
And how I wish that I had wings,
I'd fly and see magnificent things.
But I'm restricted to the ground,
It's a pity I can't glide around.

Good writers

- Use interesting words
- Use similes
- Use their senses
- Use nouns and verbs

Using Interesting Words

Recently, at a family get-together, my cousin's little boy James (age six) challenged the adults: "Okay, tell me the biggest word you can think of!" He also wanted to know the longest word in the English language. We all started guessing. Someone came up with *antidisestablishmentarianism*. Kids love learning interesting words and thinking about vocabulary:

Did You Know?
• *Stewardesses*, *reverberated*, and *lollipop* are the longest words that can be typed using only one hand on a keyboard.
• *Bookkeeper* and *bookkeeping* are the only words in the English language with three consecutive double letters.
• *Pneumonoultramicroscopicsilicovolcanoconiosis* (a lung disease) is the longest English word, according to the *Oxford English Dictionary*.

The massive popularity of the Harry Potter books comes in part from the fact that J.K. Rowling uses wordfoolery to introduce new vocabulary. Take, for example, Diagon Alley and Knockturn Alley. Say either of these as one word, and you get "diagonally" and "nocturnally." Explain to your students what these bigger words suggest. Nocturnal means "of the night," and Knockturn Alley is a dark, scary place. A diagonal angle is also an oblique angle; oblique can also mean obscure, which describes the hidden alley where young wizards shop for school supplies. Another example lies in The Mirror Of Erised. "Erised" spelled backwards becomes "desire." Read the whole inscription on the mirror backward, and it says: "*I show not your face but your heart's desire.*" (Green, 2001)

Powerful language engages the reader. In my workshops, I encourage kids to be brave and use interesting vocabulary rather than "baby words." But in *The Elements Of Style*, William Strunk Jr. and E.B. White caution writers against fancy words:

Avoid the elaborate the pretentious, the coy and the cute. Do not be tempted by a twenty-dollar word when there is a ten-center handy... (76)

Good writing has clear meaning and natural, effective language.

In your classroom, post lists of powerful words students might choose to grab the reader's attention. Help students with word choice by suggesting they look for interesting words:

> *Sometimes writers use dull words. Brainstorm words you could use that would make your writing more interesting. Revise your writing by adding precise, colorful words. An author's choice of words makes a story unique.*

Twelve Tips to Increase Word Appeal

1. Use Specific, Definite Language

Good writers use precise words and concrete details. When I pose questions to kids, they often answer in general terms such as "sad," "nice," or "good." Those words are vague and ineffective. I explain that, rather than to be wishy-washy, it's better to give a clear picture. The same holds true in writing. A *big* boy may be tall or fat, or both.

Teach kids to be specific. If they write "a tree swaying in the wind," have them specify what kind of tree. Use a thesaurus to find particular words; for example, for the word "house," a thesaurus suggests the alternatives "home," "residence," "dwelling," and "abode."

2. Avoid Overused Words

Encourage kids to find alternatives for words like *nice, fantastic, awesome,* and *great.* They are overused and imprecise.

3. Stay Away from Wordiness

Good writing is lean and vigorous. Some people use too many words to say something. Extra words lead to boring writing. Be concise. Why use six words where three will do? Teach students to overcome monotony by omitting words without changing the meaning. Look at the following examples:

> Wordy: *I was busy watching his arms—I couldn't help worrying he'd try to slip one of them around me again.* (20 words)
> Concise: *I was busy watching his arms—worrying he'd slip one of them around me again.* (15 words)

4. Avoid Repetition

Never use the same words near one another. The following examples show how, when you cut duplication, you make your writing more concise.

> Wordy: *Josh cupped his hands over his ears.*
> Concise: *Josh covered his ears.*

> Wordy: *I tried to think of something I could say that might make her feel better.*
> Concise: *I tried to say something that might make her feel better.*

5. Avoid Double Negatives

Explain to students that double negatives do not add emphasis, but rather make their writing express the opposite of what they mean. Instead of using double negatives, they should express ideas in the positive.

Wordy: *I was starting to feel less miserable.*
Concise: *I was starting to feel better.*

Wordy: *She has no cash.*
Concise: *She is broke.*

6. Use the Imperative

This strategy cuts down on repetitive use of the word "you."

Wordy: *"You take your talent for granted, young man," Mr. Watson said. "You are not hanging out with that group. You need to focus your energy on your hockey."*
Concise: *"Don't take your talent for granted, young man." Mr. Watson said. "Stop hanging out with that group. Focus your energy on hockey."*

7. Use Precise Verbs

Replace an adverb-verb combination with single, more precise verb.

Wordy: *Matt closed the cupboard door hard.*
Concise: *Matt banged the cupboard door.*

8. Omit Needless Words

Words such as *absolutely, definitely, really, very, significant, major, quite, little, rather,* and *pretty* seldom add meaning.

Wordy: *She always seemed a little sad.*
Concise: *She always seemed sad.*

Wordy: *Your mother and I were still very close.*
Concise: *Your mother and I were still close.*

Wordy: *Maybe she isn't really so bad, I said to myself.*
Concise: *Maybe she isn't so bad, I thought.*

9. Delete Redundant Words

Cut facts written elsewhere or contained earlier in a sentence.

Wordy: *Roses bloom in the month of July.*
Concise: *Roses bloom in July.*

Wordy: *Studying the subject of writing is fun.*
Concise: *Studying writing is fun.*

10. Cut Extra Prepositions

They are redundant.

Wordy: *Open up your gift.*
Concise: *Open your gift.*

Wordy: *Sit down in your seat.*
Concise: *Sit in your seat.*

11. Avoid "It" and "There" as Sentence Openers

Wordy: *It is sunny today.*
Concise: *Today is sunny.*

Wordy: *There are three things that make me happy.*
Concise: *Three things make me happy.*

"While you're writing, your best friends will be the 'cut and 'delete' keys on your computer."
—Mem Fox (memfox.com)

12. Show Instead of Tell

Telling: *It was a really hot day.*
Showing: *We were sweating from the heat.*

Writing with Description

Descriptive language creates pictures in the mind. Teach young writers to use

- Similes: Comparisons help readers relate one thing to another with which they are already familiar. Familiarity makes for easier reading.
- Nouns: Nouns give writing a concrete quality. Use adverbs and adjectives sparingly because of their abstract nature.
- Verbs: Active verbs are direct and help the writer be concise.
- Their Senses: Nothing enters the mind except through the senses. Encourage your writers to be the eyes, ears, and nose of their readers.

> ## Writing Tip from Brian Jacques
> (author of the Redwall series)
>
> "Paint pictures with words. That's the greatest advice I can give anybody... The picture will appear in the imagination so the person reading it can say, 'I can see that.'" ("Quotes")

Using Similes

Owl Moon remains one of my favorite books and an outstanding example of fine wordsmithing. Teachers often use it to demonstrate descriptive writing. Jane Yolen crafts a deceptively simple story from carefully selected words that roll off the tongue when being read aloud.

Many of the wonderful descriptions that fill *Owl Moon* are similes. Explain to students that a simile compares two unlike things. Similes often contain the word *like* or *as*. For example, the "trees stand still as statues" and the world is "quiet as a dream." Similes create pictures in the mind.

In *Owl Moon*, the young child says, "I could feel the cold, as if someone's icy hand was palm-down on my back." We all know how a cold hand feels on our back. When the girl and her father come to a clearing in the dark woods, she describes the snow as "whiter than the milk in a cereal bowl." Finally, an owl flies over and the two characters stare at one another. "Then the owl pumped its great wings and lifted off the branch like a shadow without sound." In this simile, the writer compares the bird's noiseless movement to a silent shadow.

Read poems and books full of similes at various grade levels to show students how to write them. Many primary teachers use the picture book *I'm as Quick as a Cricket* by Audrey Wood as a springboard. The language is simple, but good for introducing comparisons. For example, "I'm as slow as a snail" and "I'm as small as an ant."

Song and Dance Man by Karen Ackerman is another one of my all-time favorite picture books, and a wonderful choice for teaching similes. In this story, Grandpa dresses up in clothes from his vaudeville days—complete with top hat and gold-tipped cane—to perform tricks, play banjo, and tell jokes for his grandchildren. He taps, twirls, and laughs himself to tears on a thrown-together stage in his

I had planned to quote all of the similes in *Owl Moon*. But when I listed them in succession, I realized that there were too many—one after another. Readers need relief from so many examples. Instead, I've highlighted a few exquisite usages. You and your students will find others. Use the clue words *like* and *as*. Consider similes one example at a time to avoid brain overload; good writers use figures of speech sparingly.

attic. The narrative contains lovely similes. For example: "his voice is as round and strong as a canyon echo"; he "does a new step that sounds like a woodpecker tapping on a tree." Note the clue words *like* and *as*.

Kenneth Oppel (author of *Airborn*, *Skybreaker*, and *Starclimber*) gives older students rich models to draw on for their writing. His novels win all kinds of awards for description. As students read Oppel's books, they start to understand—and appreciate—the power of similes.

Set in an imaginary past where giant airships rule the skies, *Airborn* tells the story of Matt Cruse, the 15-year-old cabin boy of the luxury airship *Aurora*. *Airborn* contains wonderful similes. Kids can identify them in their reading. Consider these examples one at a time so you can absorb them:

> A narrow path ran like a canyon through it… (6)
> …the ocean's silvered surface, dark and supple as a snake's skin… (11)
> …we were rising into the dawn sky, sure and smooth as an angel. (23)
> Worst of all, I would start missing my father so badly that it was like a clenched fist behind my breastbone. (24)
> She's like riding a cloud. (26)
> They're eating like starved apes. (27)
> …catwalks that criss-crossed overhead like the work of some giant mechanical spider. (34)
> I felt like I had ball bearings in my stomach. (44)

Teaching Kids to Write Similes

Use the following activities to teach your students how to write similes:

1. Pick random things in the room and model how to create a simile with a specific object.

> The beam is as strong as Iron Man.
> Her lips are as red as raspberries.

Students find three items and write similes to describe each one. Make time to share them with the class.

2. Read a poem full of similes to the class. Ask students to highlight the similes. To find similes, look for the clue words *like* and *as*. Students underline the part of the sentence compares the object.

3. After students have grasped similes, they can describe themselves using similes. Read the descriptions aloud and have students guess each other's characters.

Watch Out for Clichés

Sick as a dog, fat as a pig, clear as mud… A cliché is an overused piece of language. When people like a word or phrase, they keep repeating it. Unfortunately, after a dazzling line becomes familiar, it loses its sizzle. Clichés often sound tired, like a joke people have heard too many times. The result is "ho-hum." Second-hand descriptions make a piece of writing stale. Sometimes, overused words annoy readers. Worse, they indicate that you can't think for yourself. Encourage your students to keep their language fresh and attractive. See page 89 for a list of Clichés to Avoid that you can share with your students.

Explain to students that, if writers use tired old similes, their writing sounds corny and predictable. New similes sound smart—a good reason for writers to use fresh similes whenever possible.

Using the Senses

Earlier we examined how similes enhance the writing in *Owl Moon*. Jane Yolen also uses her senses to describe things, making the experience transporting. As one reader says, "I was with the little girl and her father that night—hearing, seeing, feeling, and doing everything."

Truly, we can almost feel the cold, wintry, dry air in *Owl Moon*. We can hear the train whistle blow "like a sad, sad song" in the distance, and feet "crunch over the crisp snow." Yolen even uses onomatopoeia to make the adventure more intense. Pa calls out: "Whoo-whoo-who-who-who-whooooooo..." to simulate the call of the Great Horned Owl. We can feel the excitement and suspense when suddenly an echo threads it way through the trees.

Similarly, *Song and Dance Man* contains sensory details: "all we can hear is the silvery tap of two feet, and all we can see is a song and dance man gliding across a vaudeville stage" Karen Ackerman's images of the attic setting are pitch-perfect. Readers can visualize the steep wooden steps to the attic, the faded posters of Grandpa hanging on the walls, the cardboard boxes, the rack of Grandma's winter dresses, and the dusty brown, leather-trimmed trunk in the corner. We can smell the cedar chips and old things that fill the attic.

If I could give a gold medal for descriptive writing in novels, Kenneth Oppel would get it. Open any of his books to a random page and find lovely passages, bursting with lessons for writers. Here's one from *Airborn*, where he writes using his senses:

> With a hiss, the two doors pulled in and rolled flush along the ship's hull. The wind, the drone of the engines, and the pungent smell of the tropical sea poured into the bay. Below, starlight painted the ocean silver. (6)

We can hear the hiss of droning engines. We can feel the wind. We can smell the sea and picture the silver ocean in our mind.

Listen to Kenneth Oppel's use of sounds in *Airborn*:

> *Snap* went that first line... (13)
> With a mighty *crack* the frayed rope... (14)
> ...with a great *splash* we were dumping water ballast... (23)
> ...with a clanking *whirr*, the docking trapeze began to lower... (31)
> Miss Simpkins made a *humph* sound and gazed haughtily around... (33)

Using Nouns and Verbs

Many of us grew up mistakenly thinking that adjectives and adverbs lead to descriptive writing. Regularly, I meet language arts teachers who tell students, "Use lots of adjectives and adverbs because they are describing words. They give power to a piece of writing." In fact, the opposite is true. Too many adjectives result in wordiness and overwriting. Mark Twain once said, "As to the adjective, when in doubt, strike it out." Remember, good writing is lean and vigorous.

Nouns and verbs lead to descriptive writing. They make sentences strong. Nouns are concrete—they name people, places, and things. Verbs get the nouns moving, by adding "oomph" to the work.

Use *Song and Dance Man* to teach sensory details
- setting (page 44)
- use of nouns and verbs (page 79)
- alliteration (page 83)

Consider the use of nouns and verbs in this passage from *Song and Dance Man*:

> After wiping his shoes with a cloth he calls a shammy, Grandpa puts them on. He tucks small, white pads inside the shoes so his corns won't rub, and he turns on the lamps and aims each down like a spotlight. He sprinkles a little powder on the floor, and it's show time.

Nouns like *shammy*, *corns*, *spotlight*, and *powder* are concrete. Verbs like *tucks*, *aims* and *sprinkles* breathe life into the writing.

Owl Moon is another outstanding example of descriptive writing. Read this sentence: "Our feet crunched over the crisp snow and little gray footprints followed us." Notice Yolen's use of nouns and verbs: *Feet crunch* and *footprints follow*.

The more kids reread, the more things they notice in text. Point out the use of nouns and verbs as they occur in writing to help students read like writers.

Make a chart to record the nouns and verbs in a book. This sample comes from *Owl Moon*:

Nouns	Verbs
trees	stood
whistle	blew
meadow	moved
shadow	hooted
voices	faded
feet	crunched
footprints	followed

Look for word pictures in the books you read and discuss them with your students. When we read and reread books, we discover many lessons in them.

Showing, Not Telling

Typically young writers use the verb *to be* a lot. Look at the example from *Junie B. Jones* on page 68. Experienced writing teachers expect that from young children. They also understand writing is a developmental process. As kids become more sophisticated writers and develop a better vocabulary, they can learn to use strong verbs.

Encourage older students to write with strong verbs. The verb *to be* (*am, is, are, was, were*) lacks power. It's static. Nothing happens. Older kids can search for *am, is, are, was* and *were* in their drafts, then practice using stronger verbs.

Point out strong verbs when you read aloud to students of any age. Consider this excerpt from *Shrek*: "Shrek popped his eyes, opened his trap, and bellowed a blast of fire." *Popped, opened, bellowed…* William Steig's verbs are so strong they burst with energy.

Untold riches abound as we prepare for takeoff at the beginning of Kenneth Oppel's fantasy novel *Skybreaker*. Here's how the masterful writer describes Captain Tritus when angry—which is often:

> His fist clenched and pounded the air, his barrel chest thrust forward, and his orders shot out like a hound's bark.

Owl Moon is a wonderful metaphor for going out to find opportunities in the wide world and creates an optimistic expectation that serves children well. You can use *Owl Moon* to teach these lessons:
- getting ideas from nature (page 25) or family relationships (page 30)
- sensory details (page 79)
- setting (page 41)
- writing with nouns and verbs (page 79)
- similes (page 77)
- alliteration (page 83)
- fluency (page 91)
- visual presentation (page 109)

In the final stages of this book, I searched for *am, is, are, was* and *were* and replaced them with stronger verbs wherever possible. That made my writing more lean and vigorous.

You can use Kenneth Oppel's writing to teach the following lessons on descriptive writing:
- showing, not telling
- similes (page 77)
- sensory details (page 79)

Notice that Oppel shows us the anger, rather than telling us about it? The secret to showing instead of telling lies in the nouns and verbs: his fist *clenched* and *pounded*, his chest *thrust*, and his orders *shot* out.

Kenneth Oppel shows instead of tells in his picture books too. In *The King's Taster*, the royal chef takes Max the dog, the royal taster, on several international journeys to find a dish for the land's pickiest king. As the cook worked on the coronation feast:

> He chopped, he topped, and he tailed; he sliced and he stirred and he whisked. He cooked wild boar, peacock and venison. He baked cheese pies, rose puddings, and syllabub.

But the king picked at his food.

> In the kitchen the cook clutched at his hair. "Why doesn't the new king like my food?" he cried.

See how Oppel *shows* us the chef's frustration by clutching his hair? Again, the secret to showing instead of telling lies in the nouns and verbs: he chopped, he topped, he tailed, he sliced, he stirred, he whisked and finally the cook *clutched* at his hair.

Block Buster: Get Exercise

Stretching works well for many students, and is practical in a classroom setting. Sometimes, our minds get cloudy. When ideas just won't come, get up and move around. Go for a walk. Exercise brings oxygen to the brain and helps us think clearly again.

Record Action Words

Point out strong verbs when you read aloud. Students can also post strong verbs from their reading. Then when they turn to their own writing, they can focus on using striking verbs for better descriptions.

Writing Tip from Betsy Byars
(author of *Summer of the Swans*)

"Play up your strengths. My strength is writing dialogue and my weakness (one of them) is writing description. Therefore, I have lots and lots of talking in my books. I hardly ever physically describe my characters. I never write something like, 'He was a fat boy with blah, blah, blah.' I show that he was fat by having him talk about food a lot or raiding the fridge."

Alternatives to "Said"

Gordon Korman wrote *This Can't Be Happening!* (Book One in the Macdonald Hall series) when he was 12 years old, for a class writing assignment. Since then, he has written more than 50 novels for children and young adults, many of them humorous, action-packed stories. No wonder kids like the Macdonald Hall series. They appeal to middle graders' taste for humor. Boys especially enjoy reading

- books that make them laugh, and appeal to their sense of mischief
- fiction that focuses on action more than emotions
- books in series, such as the Macdonald Hall series, which seem to provide boys with a sense of comfort and familiarity (Ontario Ministry of Education, 2006)

Gordon Korman's nimble-witted conversational exchanges add to the appeal. He uses snappy dialogue and alternatives to the word "said":

> *"What?"* shrieked Cathy.
> *"Oh, no!"* cried Diane, appalled.
> *"Run!"* he bellowed.

Remind students that writers try to show, not tell. Whenever possible, they should *show* the tone with spoken words or actions, rather than *tell* the reader about the tone.

After sharing one of Gordon Korman's novels with your class (or any story with lots of dialogue), reread his work. Make a classroom list of all the words writers use instead of *said*. These help expand vocabulary. Share the list on page 90 with your students.

They can use these words when their overall language shows limitations in scope. But caution kids not to overuse them. When inexperienced writers use alternatives to *said* incorrectly or too often, the results distract. We understand the meaning of *said*. Unless the speaker truly *barks* or *bellows*, *said* works well.

Wordplay

"Welcome to My Seriously Joy-filled World of Words!" So opens the website of Sheree Fitch, multi-award winning author, speaker, and educator. Raised in New Brunswick, Sheree has criss-crossed Canada and other countries around the world—visiting schools and libraries, delighting children with her tongue twisters and playful use of the English language.

> I'm a writer, reciter, a speaker, a teacher, a sister, a daughter, a mother, a wife.
> A listener, a seeker, a maker of nonsense, a reader, a leader, a lipslippery fool.
> A doctor, a walker, a talk-talk-talk-talker, a giggle-glad Oma, an odd sort of soul.
> —Sheree Fitch (shereefitch.com)

Wordplay is a technique in which the writer chooses words for more than just their literal meaning. Puns, rhymes, and alliteration are common examples of wordplay. They add interest to any kind of writing.

Most writers dabble in wordplay, but some deserve special mention. Rhyme and rhythm for example, characterize Dr. Seuss's books (*Green Eggs and Ham, The Cat in the Hat, One Fish Two Fish Red Fish Blue Fish, Horton Hears a Who, How the Grinch Stole Christmas*). Roald Dahl (*James and the Giant Peach, Charlie and the Chocolate Factory, Fantastic Mr. Fox, Matilda, The Witches, The BFG*) experiments with words and invents his own vocabulary. The language is weird, but it reflects freshness and energy; for example, onomatopoeia, alliteration, pun, metaphors, and similes fill *James and the Giant Peach*.

Other children's writers identified with word play include

- Lewis Carroll (*Alice in Wonderland, Through the Looking Glass*)
- Bill Richardson (*After Hamelin, Sally Dog Little*)

- Dennis Lee (*Bubblegum Delicious, Garbage Delight, Alligator Pie*)
- Shel SilverStein (*Falling Up, A Light in the Attic, Where the Sidewalk Ends*)

Teaching Wordplay Techniques

Here are some techniques used in wordplay to share with students. Many books exist to use as models. Students can study how professional writers play with language and experiment themselves in their own writing.

Wordplay with Sounds

- Onomatopoeia: a word that sounds like it is: e.g., *Bang!*
- Rhyme: repetition of identical or similar sounds in two or more different words
- Alliteration: matching consonants sounds at the beginning of words
- Assonance: matching vowels
- Consonance: matching consonants

Wordplay with Letters

- Acronym: abbreviation formed by combining the initial components in a phrase or name
- Acrostic: a message spelled out by the first letter, syllable, or word of each line
- Anagram: rearranging the letters of a word or phrase to produce a new word or phrase

Wordplay with Word Choice

- Oxymoron: a combination of two contradictory terms
- Pun: deliberately mixing two similar-sounding words

Wordplay with Sounds and Meanings

- Homonym: words with same sound and spelling but with different meanings
- Homophone: words with same sound but with different meanings

Creating a Title

My family and I spend summers at our cottage up north. Every spring, we look forward to opening weekend—inspecting the property, raising our flag, planting the garden, dusting the kayaks, and reconnecting with our friend Doris Foster. Doris taught Latin and German in Pennsylvania. Gifted in language, she enjoys reading, writing, and public speaking. Doris always has interesting projects on the go. Once she read all seven Harry Potter books for pleasure, and brought our son a Latin dictionary so he could discover more about the words in the spells.

One year, Doris told me about a nonfiction book she read called *Eats, Shoots and Leaves* by Lynne Truss. Initially, Doris pictured a western barroom scene in which a cowboy enters, wolfs down some vittles, then pulls out his six-gun and fires a round of shots in the air. When she learned it was a funny story on bad punctuation, and that the passage referred to the diet of a herbivore, she liked the joke. To this day, Doris and I laugh about that title. Through it, we discovered a mutual love of language.

Think of how you choose a book to read. What effect does the title have on you? The name of the book either hooks your interest or loses it. Some people decide whether to read something by the title alone. Titles set the story in motion and carry a lot of responsibility.

The title is a key element in writing. Knowing the importance of a title intimidates some writers. When they try to come up with a catchy title, they often feel anxious and frustrated. Using popular books—fiction and nonfiction—as examples, teach your students ways to think of catchy titles and grab a reader's attention. Effective titles do two things:

1. Capture the reader's interest.
2. Give a clue to the topic.

Tips for Choosing Titles

- **Leave the Title Until Last:** Because thinking of a catchy title usually comes last in a writing project, encourage students to leave their title to the end. Otherwise, they may feel blocked from writing the rest of the piece. Writers often use a temporary title—we call this a "working" title.
- **Reflect Your Tone:** Don't use a humorous title if your topic is serious.
- **Be Short and To-the-Point:** First impressions matter. Titles and subtitles tease readers or give them just enough information to make them want to read more.
- **Be Indirect:** Titles can be a direct statement of your main idea or an implied one. For example, when Phoebe Gilman first wrote the Yiddish tale about a young boy named Joseph, whose grandfather sews his much-loved blanket into a jacket, a vest, and finally a button, she simply titled it "Joseph's Blanket." However, to entice her audience, she changed it to "Something from Nothing."
- **Get Help from Others:** Creating catchy titles challenge authors, editors, and publishers. Sometimes, publishers have title meetings at which everyone who has read the work brainstorms possibilities. If a writer has several titles in mind, or difficulty thinking of a good title, outsiders can help.

Try the title-meeting approach in the classroom too. When a student feels stuck thinking of a title, schedule a title meeting in your class. Ask everyone to bring title suggestions to the meeting. Record all the ideas for everyone to see. Discuss each title, and then vote on which one works best.

Brainstorming helps raise the consciousness of everyone on how to create titles. In addition to helping the writer who feels stuck, it encourages creativity and divergent thinking. Giving students opportunities to interact leads to more ideas and, ultimately, results.

Eight Ways to Come Up With Terrific Titles

1. Alliteration

Repeating initial sounds in a phrase appeals to the sense of hearing.
Horrible Histories series by Terry Deary
Greener Grass by Caroline Pignat

The Bully Boys by Eric Walters
The Wind in the Willows by Kenneth Grahame
Charlie and the Chocolate Factory by Roald Dahl
Revolting Rhymes by Roald Dahl
Backyard Birds by Robert Bateman
Call It Courage by Armstrong Sperry
Lilly's Purple Plastic Purse by Kevin Henkes
Pirate Pearl by Phoebe Gilman
The Mouse and the Motorcycle by Beverly Cleary
Runaway Ralph by Beverly Cleary
The Happy Hippopotami by Bill Martin Jr.
Maniac Magee by Jerry Spinelli
Pinky Pye by Eleanor Estes
Jack and Jill

Best-selling author Robert Munsch uses alliteration in several picture book titles:

The Paperbag Princess
Makeup Mess
Ribbon Rescue
Smelly Socks
Class Clown
Angela's Airplane
Down the Drain!
No Clean Clothes

He strings words together to give off a little buzz—a feeling of movement. And movement always adds interest for the reader. Can you hear it? These titles please the ear.

In Lemony Snicket's *Series of Unfortunate Events,* the alliteration in the titles attracts attention:

The Bad Beginning
The Reptile Room
The Wide Window
The Miserable Mill
The Vile Village
The Slippery Slope
The Grim Grotto
The Austere Academy

Where will Jack and Annie travel to next? Even Mary Pope Osborne uses alliteration in her titles of the award-winning bestselling *Magic Tree House* chapter books. These examples remind students that reading takes them to other worlds, and may give them ideas for future adventures to write:

Dinosaurs before Dark
Tigers at Twilight
Twister on Tuesday
Dolphins at Daybreak
Mummies in the Morning
Pirates Past Noon
Leprechaun in Late Winter

If your students want to add pop to their prose, have them read their work aloud. See if they can hear a buzz behind the words.

2. One Word

Often one word makes a catchy title.
Scams! by Andreas Schroeder
Hatchet by Gary Paulsen
Holes by Louis Sachar
Zoom! by Robert Munsch
Loser by Jerry Spinelli
Dust by Arthur Slade

3. Intrigue

Think of a title that relies on the element of mystery, such as Cornelia Funke's *Inkspell* or *The Thief Lord*—something that tempts the reader!
The Secret of Nimh by Robert C. O'Brien
Inkheart by Cornelia Funke
Eragon by Christopher Paolini
Looking for X by Deborah Ellis
Death in the Air (The Boy Sherlock Holmes series) by Shane Peacock

4. Rhyme

Rhyming words are fun!
Amelia Bedelia by Peggy Parish
The Cat in the Hat by Dr. Seuss
Oonga Boonga by Frieda Wishinsky
Please, Louise! by Frieda Wishinsky
Rolie Polie Olie by William Joyce
Commotion in the Ocean by Giles Andreae
Mrs. Piggle-Wiggle Betty MacDonald
The Stars from Mars by Gordon Korman
A Giraffe and a Half by Shel Silverstein
The Wonderful Pigs of Jillian Jiggs by Phoebe Gilman
Word Nerd by Susin Nielsen

5. Character

Name one or more important character.
Blubber by Judy Blume
Corduroy by Don Freeman
Chester by Mélanie Watt
Chrysanthemum by Kevin Henkes
Olivia by Ian Falconer
Shiloh by Phyllis Reynolds Naylor
Henry and Beezus by Beverly Cleary
Pippi Longstocking by Astrid Lindgren
Stuart Little by E.B. White
Matilda by Roald Dahl
Jip by Katherine Paterson

Kids can search their own writing for a favorite word or phrase that will breathe life into the title. They can also use a subtitle (an explanatory phrase) that supports the main title.

In Lemony Snicket's *Series of Unfortunate Events*, things always go badly for the Baudelaire children. Reverse psychology appears throughout the books. The narrator warns readers, "If you like happy endings, you should put this book down." By telling readers to stop reading, they want to continue.

6. Subject

Use your topic as the basis for your title.
Sharks by Seymour Simon
Animal Heroes by Karleen Bradford
Children Around the World by Donata Montanari
Growing Vegetable Soup by Lois Ehlert

7. Setting

Tell where or when the story takes place.
The Landing by John Ibbitson
Island of the Blue Dolphins by Scott O'Dell
Over in the Meadow by Ezra Jack Keats
The Summer of the Swans by Betsy Byars
Bridge to Terabithia by Katherine Paterson
The Chronicles of Narnia by C.S. Lewis

8. Question

Using a question as a title can draw in the reader.
Have You Seen Bugs? by Joanne Oppenheim
What Makes a Magnet? by Franklyn M. Branley

A Last Word on Word Choice

What do we know about good writing? Good writing includes interesting details; it helps the reader to see, hear, taste, smell, feel; it uses similes to describe; it shows instead of tells; it uses nouns and verbs.

Writing Tip from Jack Prelutsky

"READ! READ! READ! and WRITE! WRITE! WRITE! Keep a notebook and write down things you see, hear, and think about. Ideas disappear quickly unless you jot them down. When you have an idea for a poem or story, write down anything you can think of that has to do with that idea. Study your list and you'll start to see connections among certain items." ("Quotes")

Kids can look at their writing and decide:
- Have I used some strong verbs or colorful phrases that grab my reader?
- Have I chosen the most precise word?
- Have I used any unique words?
- Did I repeat common words too many times?
- Are my words clear?

Get the Words Right

Try to make your words vivid and pleasing to the ear. Conciseness strengthens writing. A lot of fine-tuning helps make your work clear, interesting, and appealing. Use this checklist as you polish your writing:

- ☐ Use a precise word rather than a general or vague word.

- ☐ Avoid overused words.

- ☐ Find one word that does the job of two words.

- ☐ Cut repetition. Never use the same words near one another.

- ☐ Express ideas in the positive.

- ☐ Add imperative—cut repetition of "you."

- ☐ Replace adverb/verb combinations with single, more precise verb.

- ☐ Omit needless words.

- ☐ Delete redundant words and facts stated earlier.

- ☐ Cut extra prepositions.

- ☐ Avoid "It" and "There" as sentence openers.

- ☐ Show instead of tell.

(adapted from Strunk and White, *The Elements of Style*)

Read your writing aloud for family or friends to test their reactions, confusion, desires, or likes and dislikes.

Clichés to Avoid

accidents will happen

add insult to injury

after all is said and done

beyond the shadow of a doubt

blushing bride

budding genius

clear as glass

dead as a doornail

depths of despair

don't have a leg to stand on

doting grandparents

eager beaver

easier said than done

easy as pie

easy come, easy go

first and foremost

get up and go

go that extra mile

good time was had by all

green with envy

happy as a lark

in a jiffy

in no uncertain terms

it goes without saying

last but not least

laugh all the way to the bank

leave well enough alone

make a long story short

needless to say

nipped in the bud

one and only

one of a kind

quick as a flash

raining cats and dogs

ready and willing

seeing is believing

selling like hot cakes

slow as molasses

snug as a bug in a rug

tough as nails

white as snow

without a moment to spare

word to the wise

you had to be there

you had to see it to believe it

(Adapted from *The Writer's Almanac*, Monday Morning Books, Inc.)

Instead of "Said"

accused	declined	pointed out
added	exchanged glances	prodded
admitted	exclaimed	prompted
agreed	explained	protested
amended	finished	put in
announced	gasped	quavered
answered	greeted	repeated
argued	grimaced	replied
asked	grinned	reminded him
barked	groaned	reminisced
bawled	growled	retorted
began	grumbled	shouted
bellowed	howled	shrugged
blurted	informed	shuffled
breathed	inquired	sighed
called	insisted	soothed
came a smothered voice	interrupted	smiled
challenged	laughed	snapped
chorused	moaned	snarled
commented	mourned	sniffled
complained	mumbled	snorted
conceded	mused	stormed
contended	muttered	suggested
continued	nodded	supplied the answer
corrected	objected	told
cried	observed	thundered
croaked	offered	warned
cut in	ordered	whispered
declared	persisted	
decided	pleaded	

Pembroke Publishers © 2010 *How Bullets Saved My Life* by Judy Green ISBN 978-1-55138-255-5

5

Fluency

… Language and word sparks and how it sounds in the reading. Cadence—all things I work with. Vital. It is challenging because I am pretty sure I hear words the way many people hear musical notes.
—Sheree Fitch (shereefitch.com)

Fluent writing has rhythm and flow. Words play to the ear, not just the eye. Sentences vary in length and structure. When a writer masters fluency, his or her phrases sound elegant and beg for reading aloud. If not, the writing lacks life and bores readers.

Ask Students to Read Aloud…

Fluency is an auditory skill as much as a writing skill. Reading aloud encourages students to read with expression. The more expressively kids read, the more likely they are to write expressively. So, promote reading to one another—in pairs, in small groups, and as a whole class.

As well, students need to hear what their own writing sounds like. In my workshops, I advise students, "Read your writing aloud to make sure it sounds right, and that you like the rhythm. Have someone else read it aloud for you as well."

Encourage kids to read their writing aloud, and ask these questions:

- Is your story easy to read?
- Do your sentences begin in different ways?
- Did you use some long and some short sentences?
- Does your writing sound smooth?
- Do you use different kinds of sentences?

Writing Tip from Betsy Byars

"Read what you have written aloud. I read my writing aloud as I go. If it doesn't sound well, it won't read well. When I first began writing, my kids would say, 'Who are you talking to in there?' because I spoke the conversations as I wrote them."

When I was a child, I learned to read with Dick and Jane books. These stories had short, awkward sentences. The characters said things like, "Run, Spot, run." Kids today are lucky to have better books to read. *Owl Moon*, the beautifully written masterpiece is a perfect read aloud for all ages, because of how Jane Yolen's words flow. No wonder so many teachers use it for fluency lessons. In this one mentor text, we see long sentences, short sentences, and how each sentence begins with a different word.

Barn Dance! by Bill Martin Jr. and John Archambault also sticks out as one of my favorites for fluency. I know right where to find it on my bookshelf. And every rereading brings a smile to my face. This fun-filled romp pulses with the rhythm of country music:

> … the skinny kid heard it…heard it faint begin…
> A *plink! plink! plink!* on the wind's violin…

Martin and Archambault build their story from a quiet moonlit night to a foot-stompin' party and back again. The words are a delight to hear, especially when all the farm animals kick up their heels to the scarecrow's fiddle playing:

> *Right hand! Left hand! Around you go!*
> *Now back-to-back your partner in a do-si-do!*
> *Mules to the center for a curtsey an' a bow!*
> *An' hey there, skinny kid! Show the old cow how!*

…And You Read Aloud, Too

Teachers can model fluency by reading aloud and sharing examples of student writing. Teach kids how to make their language smooth. They learn about fluency by reading good literature—picture books, poetry, fiction, and nonfiction—and by you reading to them. Try to be as expressive as possible. As Mem Fox, Australia's highly regarded picture book author, says, "The ups and downs of our voices and our pauses and points of emphasis are like music, literally, to the ears of young children, and they love music." (memfox.com)

Point out examples of varied beginnings, different sentence structures, and connecting words as they occur in books. Poetry is highly fluent—you should use it often. But many nonfiction samples have their own version of fluency.

"Reading aloud is not quite enough—we need to read aloud *well.*"

— Mem Fox (memfox.com)

Literature for Fluency

Throughout this book, I have mentioned great read-aloud books. The list below contains other possibilities. The language moves with rhythm and grace. Well-crafted sentences abound. The writing has cadence; it sounds like music. By reading aloud, we can train kids to *listen* to the sound of language.

Aylesworth, Jim, *Old Black Fly*
Base, Graeme, *The Sign of the Seahorse*
Bunting, Eve, *Flower Garden; My Backpack*
Fleischman, Paul, *Joyful Noise: Poems for Two Voices*
Florian, Douglas, *Bing Bang Boing*
Fox, Mem, *Time for Bed*
Grossman, Bill, *My Little Sister Ate One Hare*
Hoberman, Mary Ann, *The Llama Who Had No Pajama; The Seven Silly Eaters*
Martin, Bill and John Archambault, *Barn Dance!*
Milne, A.A., *The Pooh Story Book*
Moore, Clement C., *The Night Before Christmas*
Paulsen, Gary, *Dogteam*

Polacco, Patricia, *In Enzo's Splendid Garden*
Rigamonti, Justin, *The Pigs Went Marching Out!*
Rylant, Cynthia, *The Whales*
Dr. Seuss and Jack Prelutsky, *Hooray for Diffendoofer Day!*
Shange, Ntozake, *I Live in Music*

Writer's Tip from Mem Fox

"Constantly reread drafts aloud during the drafting process: hearing is one way of perceiving what's wrong in the text, especially in regard to rhythm." (memfox.com)

Strategies to Develop Fluency

Sheree Fitch sees herself as a storyteller, and has always had a sense of working in the oral tradition. According to Sheree, "I can tell stories in plays or verse or poems or chapter books or speech or song or novel or nonfiction…" (Fitch website) She adds, "I write long hand and then go to computer. The click of the keys interferes with cadence of sentence and word music in my head. I like the feel of pen in my hand."

Similarly, my best writing comes from stories I've told out loud and from writing longhand first. Often I write notes and phrases on scraps of paper, and then transfer everything into my laptop. I've used that method to write this book. And I read every page aloud. I think having ear training in music, being able to tell stories, doing oral presentations and being read to so much as a child all helped my writing fluency.

Year after year, students progress in their ability to develop fluency. Here are some strategies to help them.

Vary Sentence Beginnings

"Then I did my homework. Then I ate dinner. Then I went to bed." These short, choppy sentences all begin the same way. What teacher has not experienced this from a young writer? Sentences that start alike are monotonous. The writing lacks flow and is hard to read.

Six keys to good sentences:
1. Be clear.
2. Be concise.
3. Be creative.
4. Be coherent.
5. Be concrete.
6. Be correct.

Show kids how to change sentence beginnings so that they all sound different. For example, "I did my homework. After that, I ate dinner. Later I went to bed." Then compare the two versions. Which one sounds better? Teachers need to demonstrate this approach many times before most young writers practice it independently.

Vary Sentence Length

Good writers balance long and short sentences in such a way that the language flow smoothly and naturally. This variety gives writing contrast and texture. Otherwise, the writing becomes boring and readers lose interest.

What happens to fluency when all the sentences are the same length? Let's see.

I like my cat. My cat is black. His name is Blackie. He can run fast. He likes to chew shoes. His fur is soft.

Writing like this is repetitive and dull. Combine sentences, and add or eliminate details to improve the flow.

William Steig provides us with a great example of varied sentence length and structure in *Shrek*:

> Shrek wandered on. He was wondering if he'd ever meet his princess, when he saw a donkey grazing. Was this the donkey the witch had foretold? Shrek hurried over and tried the magic words: "Apple Strudel!"

Notice the short and long sentences?

Vary Sentence Structure

In addition to varying sentence lengths, the paragraph above from *Shrek* contains a statement, a question, and an exclamation. Teach kids about the four kinds of sentences:

> Declarative: makes a statement; e.g., *I play the piano.*
> Interrogative: asks a question; e.g., *Who owns this book?*
> Imperative: gives a command; e.g., *Give me your e-mail address.*
> Exclamatory: shows strong feeling; e.g., *You look great!*

Most sentences are declarative. To add interest and strength, try mixing in more question and command sentences. One word of caution: Many young writers use too many exclamation marks. In fact, that makes the statement less effective. Train students to use exclamations sparingly.

Consider Beginning a Sentence with "And"

Can you begin a sentence with "And"? Yes, even though most of us learned that a sentence should never start with a conjunction. Many teachers want aspiring writers to avoid the tendency to write in fragments, and they know that "and" at the beginning of a sentence usually indicates an incomplete sentence. When used purposefully and appropriately, starting a sentence with a conjunction can be a powerful stylistic tool.

Conjunctions form a link between one word and another. The common conjunctions are

and	nor	yet
but	or	
for	so	

Keep Sentences Short, Crisp, and Powerful

Good writing is lean and concise. When writers cram too many ideas into one sentence, readers lose interest. Every time kids use a comma or the word *and*, train them to review the sentence. Can they cut it into two sentences?

Use Active vs Passive Voice

I have a block about reading user manuals and annual reports. Usually, they numb my brain. The text either confuses me or reads as dry as chalk. Whenever any sentence sounds boring, I scan the words. Inevitably, the writer has used a passive rather than active voice.

"I want to write good sentences. It's as simple and difficult as that."

— Kevin Henkes ("Quotes")

In the active voice, the subject does something to some person or thing. For example:

Thomas picked the apples.

In the passive voice, the subject receives the action. For example: *The apples were picked by Thomas.*

See how the active voice is more direct and lively than the passive? This holds true for writing of any kind—descriptive or expository. Note that when we make a sentence stronger, it usually becomes shorter. Conciseness comes from vigor.

Encourage students to use active rather than passive voice whenever possible. Dull sentences, even in nonfiction writing, can become vigorous when you use active voice. Here are some examples:

Wordy: *Everyone was introduced to Laura's boy friend.* (passive voice)
Revised: *Laura introduced her boy friend to everyone.* (active voice)

Wordy: *Your application was accepted by the camp.* (passive voice)
Revised: *The camp accepted your application.* (active voice)

Use Short Paragraphs

Make paragraphs brief and to the point, so they're easier to read. Short paragraphs bundle your thoughts into tighter sequences, and prevent you from rambling. They are also more inviting.

Stay Clear of Dangling Modifiers

This error often happens when writers start a sentence with an *–ing* word. Look at this sentence: *While writing this book, my house got messy.*

See how I left the words *While writing this book* dangling? The sentence sounds as if my house had been writing this book. Attach dangling words to the noun, pronoun, or verb they describe in order for sentences to make sense. Here's a better version: *While I wrote this book, my house got messy.*

Avoid Interjections

Yuk! Ouch! Oops! Interjections get everyone's attention, but they interrupt the flow of writing. Teach kids to avoid them as fillers, especially in dialogue. Consider this sentence: *"Oh, here we go again," Matt yelled.*

That line would flow better, and be more exciting without the interjection: *"Here we go again," Matt yelled.*

Unless you are writing a graphic novel or action comic book, shun these interjections:

Ow!	*Ah!*	*Wow!*
Ooo!	*Yow!*	
Eeek!		

Avoid "It" and "There" as Sentence Openers

Starting sentences with *It* and *There* becomes wordy. Aim for conciseness. Also, the verb *to be* (*am, is, are, was, were*) lacks power. Teach students to use strong verbs wherever possible.

Wordy: It is cold today.
Concise: Today is cold.

Wordy: There are two things that make me happy.
Concise: Two things make me happy.

Wordy: There wasn't anything wrong with Juan.
Concise: Nothing's wrong with Juan.
More concise: Juan's fine.

Avoid Repetition

Good writers keep away from using the same words or phrases close to one another. They try not to start two consecutive sentences the same way.

If they do repeat anything, they do it for effect. Mem Fox, for example, repeats the word *not* in *Hattie and the Fox*:

"I can see a nose, two eyes, two ears, two legs, and a body in the bushes!" cries Hattie.
But no one is paying a bit of attention.
Not goose. Not pig. Not horse. Not cow.

Use Transitions

Smooth writing moves easily from one thought to the next. Transitions help pave an even path. They link ideas from sentence to sentence, and from paragraph to paragraph. By pointing out transitions when we read, we can show how writers use connecting words to join their thoughts.

Good transitions tie the current paragraph to the previous one. Encourage kids to search for transition words in their reading and to practice using them in their writing. Make connecting words accessible by posting charts on your classroom wall. See Transition Words on page 99.

We can also show kids how to use transitions as a way to move forward in time. Point out the language authors use to control time: e.g., *The next night…*; *Later that day…*; *Meanwhile…*

Use the list of Words Writers Use for Time Transitions on page 100 to help students skip forward in time.

Charts like the one on page 99 help when we post them on the classroom wall. As well, kids benefit by having their own copies of these lists to use whenever and wherever they write.

List Linking Words

Start a Linking Words bulletin board in your classroom. Assign students the job of collecting linking words to do with time. They can find and record as many words as possible from their reading books. The result will be a wonderful inventory of linking words to help in their daily writing.

Block Buster: Change the Audience

Write to a child or someone new to the subject who needs you to explain your topic slowly. This can help you see things that you otherwise take for granted or find difficult to articulate. Your writing will be stronger for it. Changing the audience can clarify your purpose, make you feel comfortable, and help you write more easily.

When the Writing Flows

In Chapter 1 we discussed writing true stories about Moments that you have experienced or witnessed. Turning experience into good writing requires fluency. Something has to happen in the story. Some feeling or emotion must be lurking behind it, in order to move the reader. Recently, I came across a story my son wrote when his Grade 7 class had to describe a critical event in their lives.

Rescue at Gold Point

Summer at Ahmic Lake was in full swing when Wayne and Marie arrived. They were towing a green and white bow-rider with a 150 horsepower inboard motor. Wayne works with my dad, and had brought up his boat for a weekend at our cottage. Ahmic Lake was three hours north of Toronto, near the village of Magnetawan.

The young couple emerged from their SUV and stood for a moment, scanning the beautiful lake—its cedar tress, blue water and rocky shore. It was a beautiful day—hot, sunny and a clear blue sky. Wayne turned to me.

"Are you going to take us for a tour of the lake?"

I stood up in a cascade of fraying rope ends. I was whipping ropes to stop them from coming apart. "Sure," I said. "But it's a bit windy out there and the water's dark." As a sailor, I knew about weather conditions. "We should wait a few minutes."

Strong winds were coming from the Northeast. Our flag was flapping at the end of the point. When it looked calmer, everyone headed down to the dock. They carried lifejackets, sunglasses and a safety bucket. My dad stayed behind to do some dock repair.

Once everyone sat down and packed away the gear, Wayne shifted his boat into reverse and carefully backed away from the dock, avoiding some nearby rocks.

"Where first?" he asked.

"Let's start with Gold Point." I motioned to the opposite shore. "You'll see an old cottage straddling two massive rocks. According to legend, it used to be a gold mine before it became a fishing camp in the 1890's."

We were about to settle down for a nice ride when the wind picked up again. Huge gusts ripped along the water's surface, blowing the tops off waves causing whitecaps. It was going to be a rough ride.

As we headed towards Gold Point, I noticed a sailboat tipped upside down, drifting towards the shore. No one appeared to be near it. "We've got to do something!" I cried. "The mast might break, or someone might be trapped underneath." Wayne steered towards it.

"Cut the engine when we get closer," I said. The motorboat rocked back and forth in the waves. Just then, a man's head popped into view from under the sailboat. He wore a pained expression on his face. I noticed blood running down his arms. He wasn't wearing a life jacket.

"Want some help?" I yelled.

"Yes please," the man said, bobbing up and down. For a second, I detected panic in his voice. I grabbed an extra lifejacket, and threw it overboard. I told him my name. "Our cottage has the red roof," I said, pointing in the distance.

"Thanks," the man said as he reached for the lifejacket. "It was such a beautiful day, I couldn't resist going out for a sail. Then, we went from dead calm to wind extremes. As I got to Gold Point I caught this gust that I couldn't handle," the man explained. "I'm glad you came by."

"So you're from around here too?" I queried.

"Yes, my place is across the bay," the man said. Winds pounded as he hauled himself up on the boat. "Can you go underneath and help me pull up the centerboard? I need it to right the boat."

I dove in the water and swam towards the overturned dinghy. It was wrenching about badly.

My mom protested. "My son is a good sailor. But he's only twelve years old, and I'm uncomfortable with him going under the boat. I'll get my husband."

My dad was standing on the dock, ready to go on a rescue mission. He had watched the whole incident with binoculars. He hopped in the bowrider. By the time they made it back to the scene, they found the sailboat upright already and me having fun in the water.

My mom hovered over me. "How did you do it?"

I shrugged. "I pushed up on the mast while he stood on the gunwhale and pulled back on the centerboard. That causes the boat to flip back over." My mom looked at the man. "Can you sail back by yourself?"

"Yes," said the man. "Thanks for your help."

We watched as he pushed the tiller away to steer home, and continued on our tour.

As his mother, I am proud of my son for his moment of kindness and bravery. And as the author of this book, I am proud of the way Cory captured that moment in writing. We see excellent fluency in his writing:

- He uses time transitions: "For a second…," "Once everyone sat down…," "As we headed towards…," "Just then…," "Then…," "By the time…," "When it looked calmer…"
- He starts most sentences with a different word to avoid repetition.
- He varies the length of his sentences. We see long sentences: "The young couple emerged from their SUV and stood for a moment, scanning the beautiful lake—its cedar tress, blue water and rocky shore." And short sentences: "Wayne turned to me."
- He varies sentence structures. We see declarative sentences: "I noticed blood running down his arms."; imperative sentences: "Cut the engine when we get closer."; interrogative sentences: "'Want some help?' I yelled."; and the occasional exclamatory sentence: "We've got to do something!"
- He keeps paragraphs brief and to the point, yet includes many interesting details.

See page 52 for the Plot Organizer used to write this piece.

In Cory's true-life narrative, all of the traits work together to support each other. He shares interesting details, making it easy for readers to imagine what was happening (see page 34); he uses a strong lead, establishes the setting, and concludes in a satisfying way (see Chapter 2: Organization); includes interesting words, and writes with nouns and verbs (see Chapter 4: Word Choice); writes in active voice and uses a variety of sentences (see Chapter 5: Fluency).

Transitions

Transition Words

Again	Besides	In other words
Along with	For example	Instead
Also	For instance	Moreover
And	Finally	Next
Another	Furthermore	Nevertheless
Anyhow	In addition	Still
As well	In any event	That is
At length	In brief	Therefore
After all	Indeed	Yet
At the same time	In fact	

Words Writers Use to Show Location

Above	Beneath	Near
Across	Beside	Off
Against	Between	On top of
Along	By	Outside
Among	Down	Over
Around	In front of	Throughout
Behind	Inside	To the right/left
Below	Into	Under

Pembroke Publishers © 2010 *How Bullets Saved My Life* by Judy Green ISBN 978-1-55138-255-5

Transitions cont'd.

Words Writers Use to Contrast Information

However	On the other hand	Opposing
On the contrary	Opposite	Unlike

Words Writers Use to Show Similarities

Accordingly	Likewise	Similarly
Like	The same	

Words Writers Use to End, Conclude or Summarize

As a result	In conclusion	Therefore
Consequently	In sum	Thus
Finally	In summary	
Lastly	So	

Words Writers Use for Time Transitions

About	Finally	Then
After	First	Third
Afterward	Later	Today
As soon as	Meanwhile	Tomorrow
At	Next	Until
Before	Second	When
During	Soon	Yesterday

Pembroke Publishers © 2010 *How Bullets Saved My Life* by Judy Green ISBN 978-1-55138-255-5

6

Conventions

> *The first draft is a skeleton…bare bones…like the first rehearsal of a play… In the second draft, I know where my characters are going, just as the director knows where his actors will move on the stage. But it's still rough and a little painful to read. By the third draft, the whole thing is taking shape.*
> —Phyllis Reynolds Naylor

Writing Conventions and Why They Matter

Writing conventions include spelling, punctuation, capitalization, grammar, and paragraphing. Proper use of conventions makes writing easy for others to read. Revision is central to clarity. After they have finished their first draft, kids can ask themselves the following questions:

- Did I use correct punctuation?
- Did I use capital letters in the right places?
- Have I proofread for correct spelling and grammar?
- Did I keep the same verb tense throughout?

In my workshops, I explain to kids that when writers use conventions correctly, three things happen:

1. Your message comes through clearly. Weak writing makes readers say, "So what?" Error-filled writing confuses and distracts readers.
2. You show respect for your readers. Readers deserve clear, error-free writing.
3. People respect quality writing. If your work is strong and error-free, people take you seriously. Your words reach people's hearts and minds. Powerful writing inspires, informs, and entertains.

Wut 2 No Abt Txt Msging

When my son attended high school, his friend phoned to arrange a carpool for band practice. Their conversation sounded like this:

Phone rings.
"Hey."
"Yep."
"'kay."
"Bye."

My son hung up, looked at his watch, and grinned. "We did that in under ten seconds!" he beamed. I looked in dismay at our boy who enjoyed his brief, barely verbal conversation. Yet today that conversation wouldn't even exist. Instead my son and his friend would text each other.

Adolescents send dozens of text messages daily. Do they still have the poise and know-how to converse, exchange ideas, and discuss? Or has abbreviated casual dialogue replaced conversation? Messaging necessitates speed and therefore choosing the shortest forms possible. Instant messaging and texting condense language to its lowest common denominator; these forms misuse grammar, sentence structure, and punctuation for the sake of brevity.

But this is still communication. We need to understand "textspeak" in all kinds of situations, because it is one of the languages our students use daily. *The Elephants of Style* author Bill Walsh says, "Language evolves, but at each instant in that evolution there will be ways of writing that will strike educated readers as ignorant." Yes, speech changes all the time, so short message lingo becomes a natural succession.

The Time for Editing

In my workshops, I offer these writing tips. The first tip may sound strange coming from an editor…

Postpone Editing

Each of us writes on two levels:

1. a creative unconscious level
2. a critical conscious level

The unconscious produces powerful words and pictures in our minds. It makes interesting and original connections. But if the critical "editor" part of your mind goes to work too soon, the unconscious shuts down. Teach spelling, grammar, punctuation, and capitalization as separate from the writing experience. If kids hear their teacher's voice run through their mind as they write, or worry about spelling, grammar, or what mark they'll get, their writing will be dull.

Let the Writing Flow

Encourage kids to unlock their unconscious minds. These ideas help:

- Brainstorm words or images about your topic. Don't stop to evaluate their worth. Keep writing down ideas. When you can't think of another word, wait a while. Often the most powerful idea will surface after you have cleared all the less valuable ideas out of the way.
- Write with music in the background. Experiment to find the style that you like.
- Give yourself permission to be emotional. If your writing begins to move you, experience the full emotion.
- Don't worry about punctuation or grammar. That can come later. Edit your writing only when you have drawn deeply from the well of your unconscious.

Are You a Honey or a Trunchbull?

Miss Honey and Miss Trunchbull are two characters in Roald Dahl's novel *Matilda*. Honey, Matilda's teacher, is kind and likes children. Trunchbull, the headmistress, exploits students' weaknesses and abuses children. Her approach hurts under any circumstances!

Once during a writing workshop with Grade 2 children, a seven-year-old boy blurted out, "I'll never be a good writer. I can't spell." I winced to hear how discouraged he felt at such a young age. That is a conditioned response. Someone—a peer, teacher, parent, caregiver, sibling, or grandparent—had made him feel like a bad writer.

Teachers play an important role in determining how individual students develop as writers. We must provide experiences that respond to their interests, needs, and learning styles.

Lucas checks the teacher's comments on his story with confusion and disappointment. He notices the words "Unclear. This is difficult to read." Further down he sees squiggles on his page signifying spelling, grammar, and punctuation problems. His mark meets the standard, but the final comment says, "Needs work."

Needs work? Lucas thought he was finished. He had tried to include interesting details and print neatly. When the teacher says "This is difficult to read," does she mean his ideas are unclear or his writing is messy? Now Lucas wonders what to do next.

Student writers face Lucas's dilemma every day. The idea of starting again overwhelms him. Lucas doesn't need to go back and start again. He needs clear communication about how to move forward—suggestions for improvement. Specific terms make it easier to write well. The success of a writing program depends on clear communication.

Moreover, if kids associate revision with something negative, or something they must go *back* and do, then it will be less appealing. Students find going back to re-do something off-putting. Give them suggestions to move forward.

Helping Kids Revise

In my workshops, I include a segment on editing. I explain to kids that each of their favorite authors shines at some parts of writing and struggles with other parts. For example, Betsy Byars, whose realistic fiction novel *Summer of the Swans* won a Newbery Medal, says her strength is writing dialogue and her weakness is description. Kenneth Oppel, whose fantasy adventure *Airborn* won the Governor General's Award, says he writes and rewrites his stories many times before he's happy with them. None of these people work by themselves. All of them get help from an editor.

When it comes to writing, teachers act in the role of an editor. So do classmates, in the form of peer editing. So do the parents, siblings, grandparents, guardians,

Effective teachers give simple objectives, clear communication, and frequent feedback.

Revise by identifying the qualities of good writing. Does the writing
- Contain vivid verbs and strong nouns?
- Create a picture in our minds?
- Include similes (comparing two things)?
- Use the senses (hearing, seeing, smelling, tasting, and feeling words)?
- Have time and place words?

and caregivers who "check" students' writing. Whenever I ask kids how they feel while somebody else reads their writing they say

Anxious
Tense
Embarrassed
Awkward
Uncomfortable
Scared
Nervous

They worry that people might make fun of them and fear others might laugh.

An editor's job is to help the writer. If you look up the word "editor" in the dictionary, you find the words *encourage, nurture, nourish, prod, prompt, suggest, support, train* and more. I tell kids that when I work as an editor, I feel like a support beam holding up a building. My job is to help make a piece of writing strong. We do that by telling the writer all the good things they're saying first—giving them credit—then making suggestions to strengthen their work. I like to think of editing as moving the writer forward: Edit → Credit.

A good editor never starts by pointing out mistakes. I can't read an author's story and then start by saying, "You spelled Samuel wrong," "None of this makes sense," or "You need to go back and fix your punctuation." A good editor begins by praising specific strengths in the content. Likewise, teachers should focus on what the writer *says*—their ideas and words—first. Start by commenting on the message. Choose specific examples from the writing that relate to content and style. For example:

Excellent organization.
Clear text.
Interesting details.

Kindness ranks as important as theoretical knowledge. When I ask kids, "What would happen if we begin by telling the writer all their mistakes?" Young children answer, "The writer will feel *sad*." Older students, whose language is further developed say, "The writer will feel *discouraged*." True. And if a writer feels discouraged, what's going to happen next?

As one ten-year-old girl in Grade 4 said, "He would lose his spirit in writing." They'll stop writing. I ask, "Do we want our favorite authors to stop writing?" Everybody shakes their head.

Young writers feel frightened and vulnerable. They feel nervous when others read their writing, afraid it may be wrong or sound stupid. Remember, elementary children are still learning to talk. They're *learning* to be good writers too. Help them feel confident enough to do their best work.

The environment for writing must be safe and nurturing. Encourage gentle but specific comments and responses. All writers are different. Find out what each writer needs and help them get it. Rather than point out what they did wrong, make suggestions for improvement. For example:

"Use *I think* less."
"Support your conclusion with details."
"Use the models provided for spelling."

"The secret of good writing is re-writing."

— Mem Fox (memfox.com)

Offer ways to move your writers forward. Children learn best when they enjoy the process. If they're anxious about their writing, that defeats the purpose. So keep it lighthearted and fun, content-rich and packed with practical skills.

Finding Errors

Two Tips for Finding Errors

1. Cover the page with another sheet of paper and read one line at a time. (Or use a ruler.) We call this line-by-line reading. This helps you concentrate on each word. Sometimes you see duplicate words, left-out letters, or punctuation problems.
2. Read the words aloud. If the reading is difficult, punctuation may be missing or incorrect. You can hear grammar errors. Well-crafted sentences want to be read aloud.

Other Secrets to Successful Proofreading

- Computers help spot common typographical errors, but hard copy works best for thorough proofreading.
- Create distance from your work. Put your writing aside for a while. This resting period might last a few minutes or a few days. However long, it allows you to read your writing with a fresh eye.
- Proofread in pairs to increase your accuracy. Get feedback. Watch your partner's face while he or she reads your work aloud. Is the wording clear, correct, and complete? Listen for repeated words or information, or places where the reader stumbles or gets lost in a sentence. You may hear parts that needs more work.

Editing Checklist

A checklist gives writers a tool for editing their work. Teachers can adapt the list on page 107 according to their needs and expectations.

Punctuation Tips

- Use dashes to introduce a word, phrase, or list. Also, use dashes to set off words and ideas.
- Use an ellipsis for omitted words.
- Use semicolons to separate independent clauses.

"I enjoy writing and it is hard. But then it's hard for everyone to write well. I have to rewrite over and over again so that on average it takes me a year to write a book."

— Avi

On Writing (and Editing)

Christopher Buckley: "The best advice on writing I've ever received was: 'Be grateful for every word you can cut.'"

Truman Capote: "I believe more in scissors than I do in the pencil."

Winston Churchill: "Broadly speaking, the short words are the best…"

Leonardo da Vinci: "Simplicity is the ultimate sophistication."

Albert Einstein: "If you can't explain something simply, you don't understand it well."

George Eliot: "The finest language is mostly made up of simple unimposing words."

Wilson Follett: "Whenever we can make 25 words do the work of 50, we halve the area in which looseness and disorganization can flourish."

Anatole France: "The best sentence? The shortest."

Robert Heinlein: "The most important lesson: writing is improved if you cut away the fat."

Samuel Johnson: "Do not use big words for little matters."

W. Somerset Maugham: "The secret of writing: stick to the point, and, whenever you can, cut."

Blaise Pascal: "The letter I have written today is longer than usual because I lacked the time to make it shorter."

Beatrix Potter: "The shorter and the plainer the better."

William Strunk: "A sentence should contain no unnecessary words, a paragraph no unnecessary sentences, for the same reason that a drawing should have no unnecessary lines and a machine no unnecessary parts."

Mark Twain: "As to the adjective, when in doubt, strike it out."

E.B. White: "Use the smallest word that does the job."

Editing Checklist

Use this checklist to help you be a better editor.

☐ My writing has a title.

☐ I put my name on the paper.

☐ I put the date on my paper.

☐ Each sentence starts with a capital.

☐ Each sentence ends with punctuation.

☐ I checked for missing words.

☐ My sentences are in the right order.

☐ I left spaces between my words.

☐ Each sentence begins with a different word.

☐ I checked my spelling.

Pembroke Publishers © 2010 *How Bullets Saved My Life* by Judy Green ISBN 978-1-55138-255-5

7

Visual Presentation

> *Being a graphic designer allowed me to build the story visually with charts, lists and graphics before writing the actual text.*
> —Mélanie Watt (Watt, 2009)

Presentation is the finished look of writing when it is ready to share. In other words, it is the overall appearance of "published" writing. Explain to students that clarity and neatness play an important part in effectively getting their message across to the reader. Show them how to

- Indent paragraphs and leave spaces between words.
- Double-space, using a readable font or neat handwriting.
- Add title and page numbers.
- Include pictures connected to text.
- Make sure papers are clean, unwrinkled, and free of smudges.

In Grade 4 my son Cory borrowed my computer to type his story. After an hour or so, I checked to see how he was doing. When I looked at the screen, I noticed two spaces separating each word.

"What are you doing?" I asked.

"Teacher said to double-space," he replied.

"Double-space means to skip lines, not to put two spaces between words." I offered.

Teachers need to explain and show by example what they mean. Ever since then, I demonstrate double-spacing in my workshops. First, I use black markers and lined chart paper to list the elements of good writing. Then I write a passage that we edit together. I always leave a space between each line and explain to kids that double-spacing is the easiest to read—and the easiest to revise. Show kids how to double-space so they can practice in their writing.

Even if we use precise words, unique ideas, and correct sentences, we need to show the elements of presentation to make our writing inviting. Elements of presentation include:

- Appropriate use of fonts and sizes
- Appealing use of white space
- Use of bullets, numbers, and sidebars that help readers access content
- Effective integration of text and illustrations, photos, charts, graphs, maps, and tables
- Skillful and tasteful use of colors

What You Can Do

- Show students examples of good presentation in books, magazines, brochures, and displays.
- Point out specific elements that make the model work.
- Ask students to bring in examples of good presentation.

In *Do Unto Otters: A Book About Manners* by Laurie Keller, each spread teaches the value of a different type of behavior. Visual and verbal gags fill the pages. Kids enjoy the references to other books hidden in the margins and back cover. Fun fact: Keller always puts one of the characters from her previous book in the new one. "Each page burst with colorful illustrations and is scattered with words of different sizes and fonts. This simple story is certain to appeal to children." (Atmur, 2007)

Increasing Readability

Teachers can demonstrate readability by using black markers on white backgrounds and printing legibly. Model and guide how readability smoothes the path for the reader.

1. White Space: White space relaxes the eyes. Relaxed eyes make for relaxed minds. Encourage students to double-space their writing and to leave white space in margins.
2. Graphics: Graphics include photos, illustrations, tables, graphs, and charts. They demonstrate ideas. They also break up text and add to the white space. In nonfiction writing, headings and subheadings help organize information. Bulleted points and numbered lists help too.
3. Go Short: Shorter is easier to read. Shorter paragraphs, shorter sentences, shorter words...
4. Black on White: Black letters on white background offer high contrast and are easy to read.
5. Use a Readable Font and Size: Text should look pleasing, but never distracting. The standard size for body text is 12 points.

Visual Elements

Fonts

Times New Roman is a good choice for body text, because the letters have serifs—those tiny "ticks" you see on the tips of letters that almost join them to the next letter. Explain to your students that serifs help our eyes move from left to right, making words flow smoothly so that the text is easier to read. Encourage kids and other members of the school community to use serif fonts for body text.

Sans serif fonts do not have the tiny ticks on the tips of letters. Sans serif fonts look clean, and make great headings and titles. Either serif or sans serif fonts work well in headings.

serif   sans serif

Headings

Teachers can use nonfiction books to show how designers treat headings. Major headings are bigger and bolder than minor headings. Headings help organize information and catch the reader's attention. Above all, aim for readability.

Italics

Use *italic* type to
- Name titles of books, movies and plays. For example: *Elijah of Buxton* won awards.
- Make words stand out. For example: I will *always* remember him.
- Identify a word or phrase that you are discussing. For example: What is a *serif*?

However, use italics sparingly or you will distract the reader.

Spaces After a Period

Use only one space after any punctuation. Years ago, in typing class, we learned to type two spaces after a period. That rule no longer applies. Computers automatically use proportional fonts and justification, which create the proper white space between sentences. So now, teach students to use only one space between sentences.

Bullet Points and Lists

Bullet points are a popular tool when writing nonfiction. Writers like bullet points because they draw attention to important information. Readers like bullet points because they are visually appealing and make it easy to find specific information. Teach students to use a maximum of five bullets per list. Any more than five and you lose the reader. As you explain how to use bullet points in nonfiction writing, keep the following tips in mind:

- Keep lists brief.
- Begin with action verbs when possible.
- Make verb tenses consistent.
- Limit your list to five items, if possible.
- Conclude with at least one sentence to give your readers a sense of completeness. Ideally, the wrap-up sentence emphasizes the importance of the list itself.

Remember to use bulleted lists sparingly. No one wants to read more bullets than narrative. Bullets are like spices; use them in moderation.

Looking In from the Outside

People say, "You can't judge a book by its cover." But everybody *does*. In my workshops, I teach kids about visual presentation. We look at the covers of books on display. Most often, we see two basic designs:

1. Title printed along the top with artwork below. The art contains no border; it flows off the page.
2. Title printed along the top with artwork below. The art is enclosed by a border.

Show how color, scale, and balance can work together to create eye-catching covers. Kids can look for covers they like best then practice these skills in their title pages.

I show kids a book such as *Chester* by Mélanie Watt and ask, "What do you like about the cover?" Chester, the intrusive cat, features prominently. As a character, he's bold and fearless. He's also kind of a loner. He's so big he takes up most of the page, and he faces the readers. We discuss how the large illustration and large-size print in the title—one color, one word—match Chester's self-centred personality. I point out how Mélanie Watt centres the title on the page and uses bright letters on a pale background. That contrast makes the words easy to read. In addition, she uses child-like lettering in upper/lower case that goes with Chester's character. A reviewer says, "The creative illustrations and font style and color which show Chester's personality and naughtiness made me laugh out loud." (Shelley, *LibraryThing*)

Have your class study book covers. Use the books in your classroom library to teach about

- Using large-size print for titles, and centring the title on the page
- Contrasting the letter colors with background colors for readability
- Using smaller-size print for the writer's name
- Featuring the main character (or theme) in an active pose or facing readers
- Using colors and styles complementary to the topic

Choosing Title Fonts

Title fonts should match the meaning of the topic. (Imagine writing about medieval times with futuristic letters!) Interesting letter styles help bring a topic to life. Above all, however, the letters must be readable and the words recognizable. Talk to students about using visual characteristics that match their topic.

Since many words have their own visual characteristics, kids can choose a lettering style to give that word personality. Specially designed words, like these ones by illustrator/author Mark Thurman, add interest to the text:

Kids can choose words from the list below. Then they can add impact by hand-drawing lettering styles or choosing interesting fonts on the computer to match their word.

Noodles	Fire	Bubble
Fast	Electricity	Steel
Rainforest	Cats	Quick
Space	Blob	Monsters
Trees	Cheese	Big
Lightning	Shake	Convicts
Roads	Skyline	Humor
Spooky	Shatter	Tense
Grace	Wool	Thin
People	Tall	Rocks
Supernatural	Writing	Water
Clouds	Fear	Fairies
Waste	Pollution	Fat

Title Do's and Don'ts

- Never underline or put titles in quotations. Use boldface.
- Do not place a period at the end of the title. However, do use a question mark or an exclamation point if warranted.
- Centre the title. Capitalize the first letter of the first word and all other important words. Instead of *LUMPS, BUMPS, AND BODY SLAMS,* try *Lumps, Bumps, and Body Slams.*

A Final Word on Final Copy

Throughout this book, I have recommended using *Owl Moon* by Jane Yolen to teach a variety of writing lessons. Teachers can also use it to show pleasing presentation. On the cover, big blue letters show the title *Owl Moon.* The color of the letters blends with the artwork. Smaller black letters show the author's and illustrator's names.

Inside *Owl Moon,* we see black words on white background. Explain to kids, "Black on white provides high contrast. That helps readability." Encourage them to use black on white in their writing. Explain that each page layout uses a double-page spread, which means the picture extends across two pages. This adds the effect of motion by having the reader's eyes move from one page to the other.

When students prepare their writing for sharing, they should know how illustrations and captions give a fuller idea about the writing. Are there graphs, charts, maps, diagrams? What do they show? Graphic aids can sum up some kinds of information more clearly than words alone can.

Not all student writing ends up as "good copy," but "publishing" their best work encourages students.

Conclusion

Knowing how to write well is indispensable in life. Good writing strategies help set students up for success in all subject areas. Using first-rate authors as role models, teachers can demonstrate writing excellence. Make time for kids to practice. Becoming a good writer will serve kids well both in and out of school.

Lynne Shuttleworth, a Grade 4 teacher, engages her class in a medieval study. She gives kids the opportunity to choose a topic they find interesting, and an outline to help frame their research. After they read about their topic, they make a web with research questions and subtitles. Then they write information in point form—along with charts, graphs, labeled diagrams, and timelines—a project plan, and a work log. As Stephanie Harvey says, "Methodical organization is essential to accurate nonfiction writing." (*Nonfiction Matters*: 144)

My son chose the topic War Strategies in Medieval Times. He relished the thought of building a model of a castle with towers, tunnels and trebuchets to support his written material. First, he created a web:

In *Moon and I*, Betsy Byars tells us the way she writes her books. The ways in which she conducts her research are so interesting and helpful that you might want to read the book aloud at the onset of a research project.

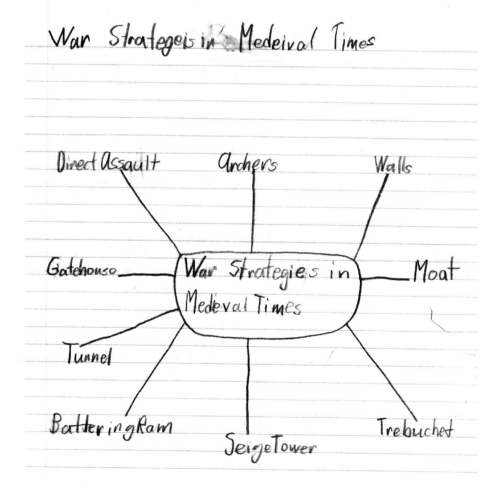

Next, he read and wrote information for each subtitle in point form. For example:

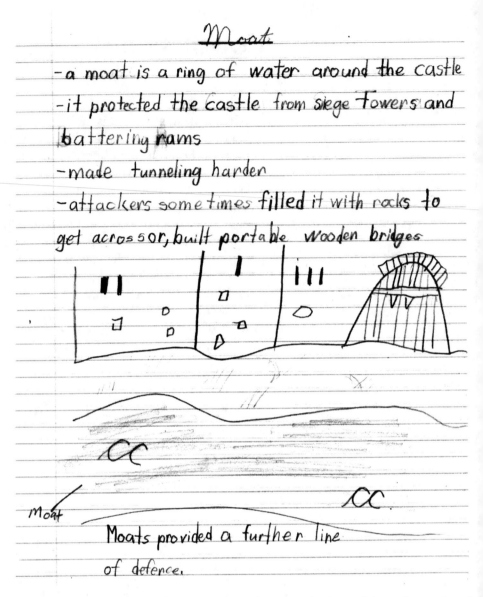

Moat

- a moat is a ring of water around the castle
- it protected the castle from siege towers and battering rams
- made tunneling harder
- attackers sometimes filled it with rocks to get across or, built portable wooden bridges

Moat

Moats provided a further line of defence.

Along with his point-form notes, he drew diagrams, built models, and completed a work log. Cory incorporated his research to write an oral presentation. He assumed the role of a French leader and made his class audience the troops:

"Bonjour! Je suis le marquis de Karaba. I have orders from the king to gain control of more land. To do this, fellow soldiers, we must launch a siege. Today we will discuss strategies to fight our siege: Secret tunnels, terrifying trebuchets, battering rams… Our goal is to do away with the English garrison who control the land around their stone fortress.

First, let us look at the castle. They have a moat, a ring of water around their castle. It protects them from battering rams and will make tunneling hard for us. We will have to fill it up with rocks to get across, or build portable wooden bridges.

If we get across the moat, their gatehouse (castle entrance) is our next target. I'll warn you about the portcullises. Those iron covered wooden grills move up and down. They protect our enemies. If we break in, they might lower the gate and trap us.

You know, castle walls used to be made of wood and we could easily burn them down. Now the walls are made of stone. Be careful of the corner tower. From there they can see our moves.

Of course, both armies will have archers. Our enemies have the advantage shooting from the castle..."

When we look closely, we begin to notice that all the traits lend themselves to this piece. I know that the organizing strategies above made writing easier for Cory, and helped lead to better results. His presentation follows a logical sequence with an introduction, body and conclusion. He chooses interesting words such as *portable wooden bridges* and *secret tunnels*. As well, he practices using devices like alliteration (*terrifying trebuchets*) to make his writing sound interesting. After he outlined every war strategy, he ended this way:

"Now that we have explored all of the war strategies in detail, I want you discuss your plans. Do whatever it takes to gain control of more land. Let the battle begin!"

In the end, Mrs. Shuttleworth commented "Linking the information the way you did made a very enjoyable presentation." From this experience, Cory gained valuable research and planning strategies, the chance to practice writing skills—and knowledge in the content area. And we see how all the traits support good writing.

Acknowledgments

Mary Macchiusi and I have worked together in the book business for over 25 years. She has helped make my career what it is today. This book evolved because many people, starting with Mary encouraged me along the way. I have heard the voices of family, friends, kids, colleagues and mentors giving their thoughts. More than anything, I hope my writing is relevant to you, the audience.

The great inventor Thomas Edison once said

> None of my inventions came by accident. I see a worthwhile need to be met and I make trial after trial until it comes. What it boils down to is one per cent inspiration and ninety-nine per cent perspiration.

Edison's quote speaks to me. Once I saw a worthwhile need to meet, and began writing this book, I made trial after trial until it came. For me, too, this project has been one per cent inspiration and 99 per cent perspiration.

Thanks to David Booth for writing the Foreword. One September, the Toronto Catholic School Board hosted a gathering to kick-off the school year. They asked David and me to speak. I remember the wording on their program: "David Booth for Inspiration ~ Judy Green for Information." David's experience and wisdom support much of this book.

Growing up knowing how much writing meant to my grandmother gave me an appreciation for writing and a respect for those who write. Yet when my mother credited Grandma with providing inspiration for my work, I didn't see the connection. Not until a friend explained, "You are her posterity!" did I realize the importance of my grandmother's legacy. How fitting it is to find family treasures and my craft merge in this endeavor.

Thanks also to my nieces, Sophie and Laura, for input and samples; thanks to my sister Heather, their mom, and to John, their dad—also both writers — for couriering copies of their work. Thanks, too, to Michelle Scott for providing samples of her writing.

Special thanks to Doris Foster who shared her insights about young writers, writing and language. As I struggled through some rough spots along the way, Doris's encouragement helped, and her feedback was invaluable. Doris became a catalyst for me. The experience came full circle when she e-mailed me one day to say, "The examples fascinate me. If I reincarnate, I want to be a children's librarian!"

My appreciation to Pembroke Publishers and Kat Mototsune, whose editorial work and helpful suggestions pushed me to the finish line.

Imagine: ten years have passed since I wrote my last book. In that time, I have met hundreds of teachers and students who have infused me with new ideas. Thanks to the teachers, principals and kids in my workshops – I value the thoughts, opinions and enthusiasm they bring to our discussions. My workshops evolve as students give me insight toward their feelings as readers and writers.

Thanks to all the authors I've worked with and those whose writing I've admired from afar. I learned a lot about the craft of writing by studying their work. As an editor and writer, I strive to put theory into practice. And as the author of this book I've deconstructed the craft of writing for teachers and students.

Thanks also to my friends who ran errands, picked up library books, and spurred me on with their support. Some days, when I felt I had no steam left, these people helped move me forward – each in their special way. What wonderful friends!

Thanks once again to my husband, Jim, for tolerating stacks of books and papers taking over the house, for reading, for listening, and smiling patiently through it all.

Finally, thanks to our son Cory who, as a typical tech-savvy student, showed me how to create indexes and charts on a computer; as a trivia buff, contributed facts to the sidebars, which add another dimension to the book and made for interesting conversation; as a ski coach, helped me draw parallels between teaching skiing and teaching writing; and as a language learner, provided all kinds of writing samples from his years in elementary school. He features prominently in the book, although he'd rather not know it.

References and Resources for Further Reading

Atmur, Donna (2007) "Review of *Do Unto Otters*" in *School Library Journal Review* at http://www.librarything.com/

Avi, "Quotes from Authors on Writing" *Slideshare* at http://www.slideshare.net/pkrambeck/quotes-from-authors-on-writing

Booth, David (2009) *Whatever Happened to Language Arts?* Markham, ON: Pembroke.

Bourgeois, Paulette "Kids Can Press - presents Author Paulette Bourgeois" at http://www.kidscanpress.com/Canada/CreatorDetails.aspx?CID=20

Brown, Ian (2010) "The Idea of Canada, on Display" in *The Globe and Mail*, February 14.

Byars, Betsy at http://www.betsybyars.com/writing.html

Calkins, Lucy (1994) *The Art of Teaching Writing*. Portsmouth, NH: Heinemann.

Culham, Ruth (2003) "6 +1 Traits for Revision" in *Scholastic Instructor Magazine*, October.

Dorfman, Lynne R. and Rose Cappelli (2007) *Mentor Texts: Teaching Writing Through Children's Literature, K–6*. Portland, ME: Stenhouse.

Dorfman, Lynne R. and Rose Cappelli (2009) *Nonfiction Mentor Texts: Teaching Informational Writing Through Children's Literature, K–8*. Portland, ME: Stenhouse.

Fitch, Sheree at http://www.shereefitch.com/

Fitch, Sheree (2010) Interview by Kerry Clare, "Author Interviews @ Pickle Me This: Sheree Fitch" at http://www.picklemethis.com/2010/06/14/author-interviews-pickle-me-this-sheree-fitch/

Fletcher, Ralph and JoAnn Portalupi (2007) *Craft Lessons, 2nd Edition: Teaching Writing K–8*. Portland, ME: Stenhouse.

Fletcher, Ralph and JoAnn Portalupi (2001) *Nonfiction Craft Lessons: Teaching Information Writing K–8*. Portland, ME: Stenhouse.

Fox, Mem and Lynn Wilkinson (2009) *English Essentials: the wouldn't-be-without-it guide to writing well*. South Yarra, AU: Macmillan Education.

Fox, Mem at http://www.memfox.com/welcome.html

Gertridge, Allison (2002) *Meet Canadian Authors & Illustrators, Revised Edition*. Markham, ON: Scholastic Canada.

Green, Judy (1999) *The Ultimate Guide to Classroom Publishing*. Markham, ON: Pembroke.

Green, Judy (2001) "Harry Potter Hidden Meanings Revealed!" in *Kidsworld*, Volume 9, Issue 4.

Harvey, Stephanie (1998) *Nonfiction Matters: Reading, Writing, and Research in Grades 3–8*. Portland, ME: Stenhouse.

Haworth-Attard, Barbara (2004) "Tips for Winning Story Contest," in *Toronto Star Starship: Just For Kids,* D16, Sunday, May 16.

Henkes, Kevin, "Meet Kevin" at http://www.kevinhenkes.com/meet/interview.asp

Henkes, Kevin, "Quotes from Authors on Writing" *Slideshare* at http://www.slideshare.net/pkrambeck/quotes-from-authors-on-writing

Jacques, Brian, "Biography" at http://www.puffin.co.uk/nf/Author/AuthorPage/0,,1000020670,00.html#QUE

Jacques, Brian, "Quotes from Authors on Writing" *Slideshare* at http://www.slideshare.net/pkrambeck/quotes-from-authors-on-writing

Korman, Gordon (2004) "Author of the Month" in *Scholastic Book Club: Arrow.*

"Make a Diary" *Scholastic Canada - Dear Dumb Diary* at http://www.scholastic.ca/titles/deardumbdiary/game/diary.htm

Matas, Carol (2003) "Author Insight" in *Scholastic Book Club: Arrow.*

Munsch, Robert (1993) Interview by Judy Green, "Interview with Robert Munsch" Author Profile. Toronto, ON: Annick.

Naylor, Phyllis Reynolds, "Quotes from Authors on Writing" *Slideshare* at http://www.slideshare.net/pkrambeck/quotes-from-authors-on-writing

Nixon, Joan Lowery, "Quotes from Authors on Writing" *Slideshare* at http://www.slideshare.net/pkrambeck/quotes-from-authors-on-writing

Numeroff, Laura (1998) "Spotlight" in *Scholastic Book Club: SeeSaw.*

Ontario Ministry of Education (2006) *Me Read? No Way! A Practical Guide to Improving Boys' Literacy Skills.* Available at http://www.edu.gov.on.ca/eng/document/brochure/meread/meread.pdf

Oppel, Kenneth at http://www.kennethoppel.ca/faq.htm

Park, Barbara "KidsReads.com - Junie B. Jones by Barbara Park" at http://www.kidsreads.com/series/series-junie-author.asp

Parravano, Martha (2010) "Reading Three Ways" *The Horn Book* at http://www.hbook.com/resources/parents/parravano_reading3ways.asp

Paulsen, Gary "Quote by Gary Paulsen" *goodreads* at http://www.goodreads.com/quotes/show/154109

Perry, Donald, "Quotes from Authors on Writing" *Slideshare* at http://www.slideshare.net/pkrambeck/quotes-from-authors-on-writing

Prelutsky, Jack "My Biography" *Writing with Writers - Scholastic.com* at http://teacher.scholastic.com/writewit/poetry/jack_meet.htm

Prelutsky, Jack, "Quotes from Authors on Writing" *Slideshare* at http://www.slideshare.net/pkrambeck/quotes-from-authors-on-writing

Riggs, Ransom (2007) "How to Beat Writers Block" *Mental Floss Blog* at https://www.mentalfloss.com/blogs/archives/8864

Rowling, J.K. (2001) "Spotlight" in *Scholastic Book Club: ArrowTAB.*

Scrimger, Richard at http://www.scrimger.ca/home.htm

Slade, Arthur, (2004) "Tips for Winning Story Contest," in *Toronto Star Starship: Just For Kids*, D16, Sunday, May 16.

Spandel, Vicki (2004) *Creating Writers Through 6-Trait Writing Assessment and Instruction.* Columbus, OH: Allyn & Bacon.

Spandel Vicki and Jeff Hicks (2002) *Write Traits® Student Traitbook.* Wilmington, MA: Houghton Mifflin.

Spinelli, Jerry (2000) "Spotlight" in *Scholastic Book Club: ArrowTAB*, March.

Spinelli, Jerry, "Quotes from Authors on Writing" *Slideshare* at http://www.slideshare.net/pkrambeck/quotes-from-authors-on-writing

"Story Exchange" *CBC Vinyl Café with Stuart McLean* at http://www.cbc.ca/vinylcafe/story_exchange.php

Strunk, William and E.B. White (1979) *The Elements of Style*. New York, NY: Macmillan.

Thurman, Mark and Emily Hearn (2010) *Get Graphic! Using Storyboards to Write and Draw Picture Books, Novels or Comic Strips*. Markham, ON: Pembroke.

Trottier, Maxine (2004) "Tips for Winning Story Contest" in *Toronto Star Starship: Just For Kids* D16, Sunday, May 16.

Truss, Lynn (2003) *Eats, Shoots and Leaves: The Zero Tolerance Approach to Punctuation*. London, UK: Profile Books.

Van Allsburg, Chris, "Quotes from Authors on Writing" *Slideshare* at http://www.slideshare.net/pkrambeck/quotes-from-authors-on-writing

Walsh, Bill (2004) *The Elephants of Style: A Trunkload of Tips on the Big Issues and Gray Areas of Contemporary American English*. New York, NY: McGraw-Hill.

Walters, Eric (2000) King City Public School Visit, York Region Board of Education.

Watt, Mélanie (2008) "Lessons from the Nut Tree: An Interview with Mélanie Watt" *Shelf Elf: read, write, rave* at http://shelfelf.wordpress.com/2008/04/16/lessons-from-the-nut-tree-an-interview-with-melanie-watt/

Watt, Mélanie (2009) "Interview with Mélanie Watt" *The Cybils Children's and Young Adult Bloggers' Literary Awards 2009* at http://www.cybils.com/2007/03/an_interview_wi.html

Weihardt, Ginnie (1996) "All About Author Avi" *About.com: Fiction Writing* at http://fictionwriting.about.com/od/interviews/p/avi.htm

The Writer's Almanac: Tips and Resources for Every Kind of Writing (1999) Ashland, OH: Monday Morning Books.

Yolen, Jane at http://janeyolen.com/for-kids/

Children's Books

Picture Books

Song and Dance Man by Karen Ackerman
Miss Nelson is Missing! by Harry Allard and James Marshall
Proud as a Peacock, Brave as a Lion by Jane Barclay
The Memory String by Eve Bunting
Miss Rumphius by Barbara Cooney
The Story about Ping by Marjorie Flack
Hattie and the Fox by Mem Fox
Something from Nothing by Phoebe Gilman
Chrysanthemum by Kevin Henkes
Lilly's Purple Plastic Purse by Kevin Henkes
Amazing Grace by Mary Hoffman
Do Unto Otters: A Book About Manners by Laurie Keller
Barn Dance! by Bill Martin Jr. and John Archambault
More Pies! by Robert Munsch
The King's Taster by Kenneth Oppel
Junie B., First Grader: Aloha-ha-ha! by Barbara Park

The True Story of the 3 Little Pigs by Jon Scieszka
Where the Wild Things Are by Maurice Sendak
A Bad Case of Stripes by David Shannon
Doctor De Soto by William Steig
Shrek! by William Steig
Alexander and the Terrible, Horrible, No Good, Very Bad Day by Judith Viorst
Chester by Mélanie Watt
Chester's Masterpiece by Mélanie Watt
Please, Louise! by Frieda Wishinsky
You're Mean, Lily Jean by Frieda Wishinsky
Owl Moon by Jane Yolen
Hey, Al by Arthur Yorinks

Novels

Dear Dumb Diary by Jim Benton
Superfudge by Judy Blume
Summer of the Swans by Betsy Byars
Artemis Fowl by Eoin Colfer
Elijah of Buxton by Christopher Paul Curtis
The BFG by Roald Dahl
Matilda by Roald Dahl
Everything on a Waffle by Polly Horvath
How It Happened in Peach Hill by Marthe Jocelyn
Alice, I Think by Susan Juby
Diary of a Wimpy Kid by Jeff Kinney
Schooled by Gordon Korman
Something Fishy at Macdonald Hall by Gordon Korman
This Can't Be Happening! by Gordon Korman
Ticket to Curlew by Celia Barker Lottridge
Gathering Blue by Lois Lowry
The Giver by Lois Lowry
Jesper by Carol Matas
Sarah, Plain and Tall by Patricia MacLachlan
Out of the Cold by Norah McClintock
Airborn by Kenneth Oppel
Darkwing by Kenneth Oppel
Firewing by Kenneth Oppel
Skybreaker by Kenneth Oppel
Starclimber by Kenneth Oppel
Death in the Air by Shane Peacock
Eye of the Crow by Shane Peacock
Holes by Louis Sachar
Loser by Jerry Spinelli
Maniac Magee by Jerry Spinelli
Wringer by Jerry Spinelli
The Hobbit by J.R.R. Tolkein
The Bully Boys by Eric Walters
Camp X by Eric Walters
Charlotte's Web by E.B. White

Nonfiction

Backyard Birds: An Introduction by Robert Bateman
Awesome Egyptians by Terry Deary & Peter Hepplewhite
Horrible Histories series by Terry Deary & Peter Hepplewhite
Junk Drawer Jewelry by Rachel Di Salle and Ellen Warwick
Remembering John McCrae by Linda Granfield
Skating for Power and Speed by Sean Rossiter and Paul Carson
Scams! by Andreas Schroeder
Terry Fox: A Story of Hope by Maxine Trottier

Index